YOU HAVE
THE RIGHT TO
TALK
TO
ALIENS

SEV TOK

Acknowledgements

A heart-felt thank you to my best girlfriends who weave a strong safety net for me. I have admiration and gratitude for my parents, Sevim & Ergun Tok, for coming to America and encouraging my sister and me to expand our minds. An eternal, love-filled thank you to Patrick who supports me in my quest for authenticity. "Why limit your exoticness?" Patrick once asked me, fueling my desire to discover and uncover the most genuine version of myself, which I present to you through this book.

TABLE OF CONTENTS

GALACTIC VISITOR

1973-1975, Crofton, Maryland

"Yay! He is back!" I think to myself as my eyes look up towards the sky. Watching him descend, I see the details of the bottom of his spacecraft. It is dark gray with grooves in the metal and blinking, multi-colored lights. The craft hovers silently above my head. There is no fear inside me, only true joy, for I miss him.

None of his visits are alike. His craft approaches from a different direction each time. Our conversations seem like chit chat but have a deeper purpose. He is checking up on me. He asks me how I am doing. I always tell him I am fine. It is just he and I standing beside his craft. This is my private time with someone whom I trust and love. He is not of Earth though.

He looks human, but his ears are a little different. They are larger than human ears and slightly almond-shaped. His hair is dark and short but not a buzz cut. He looks young to me, as if he is in his twenties. He wears the same thing each time. It is a uniform of dark-colored clothes. I cannot tell if the shirt is attached to the pants or not. He walks out the spacecraft's door and down a staircase to greet me, as I await on the ground.

My first memories of him are when I am in fifth grade, at the age of ten. We continue our visits until I am twelve years old. I lose count of how many times he checks up on me.

There is a final visit, much different than all the others. In this last visit, it is no longer just the two of us. I am surrounded by other children. We are all about the same age. We are silent as his craft lifts off and soars out of our line of sight. When I can no longer see the spaceship, my attention lands on the children around me, whom I do not know and do not speak with. We stand beside one another, silently digesting the fact that our beloved friend just said good bye to all of us. We are left to do our work.

My re-entry is always a shock to my system. What am I doing here in this bedroom, in this life? This life feels like pretend. What is real is my friend in the spacecraft. I tell no one about my galactic friend's visits, not even my parents.

Why am I left behind? Where does my galactic friend come from? Who are the other children? These questions get swept to the back of my mind. I have to deal with the reality of the present moment. I have to get dressed, go to fifth grade, and pretend to be something other than what I really am.

ALIEN NEIGHBORHOOD

I used to be a card-carrying alien. I traded in my green-colored alien card for a piece of paper declaring my American citizenship in 1995. According to the IRS, an alien is someone who is not a U.S. national or U.S. citizen. I am not an alien anymore, under the laws of the U.S. government. However, when I visit another country, I am an alien to that country. I am also an alien to any being not from Earth. We are all aliens in the eyes of someone.

If you believe Earthlings are the only intelligent beings in all the galaxies, you are in for an awakening for two reasons. First, we are not all that intelligent. If you insist we are, then why can't we explain gravity, how bees fly, what dreams are, how the Great Pyramid of Giza was built, and why dogs prefer to poop facing north or south?

Second, mathematic probability supports that we are not alone. Scientists estimate there are ten trillion galaxies in the universe. Using data from the Kepler telescope, there are an estimated nineteen sextillion stars similar to our Sun with a planet similar to Earth.[1] What are the odds that humans are the only

---

[1] Forbes.com, Nov. 2017, The Number of Earth-Like Planets in the Universe is Staggering - Here's the Math.

advanced species in the galaxy? One in 60 billion.[2] There is a better chance you will get hit by lightning, eaten by a shark, date a supermodel, win the Powerball, or achieve sainthood than the chance that humans are the only advanced lifeforms in the universe.[3]

We may not be the most intelligent beings, but we are intelligent enough to desire more intelligence. And that is where the aliens come into play. Imagine what life on Earth could be like if we freely engaged in communication with beings from other planets. What would they teach us? If we formed alliances with other intelligent life we could learn to create a world where there is free energy, no war, no hunger, no killing, teleportation, a cleaner planet, and a healthier population.

Maybe you think alien life will destroy us. If they were out to burn us to bits, it would have happened already. It is not aliens who pose the fear of wiping out humanity, it is humans. We are a mean bunch. We like to kill. We like to take over. We like to steal and we like to control.

What intelligent alien would intentionally land here to risk death due to our ignorance and hostile attitude? For those

---

[2]Airspacemag.com, May 2016, The Odds That We're the Only Advanced Species in the Galaxy are One in 60 Billion.

[3]Bostonglobe.com, August 2017, These Extremely Rare Things are More Likely to Happen to You Than Winning the Powerball Jackpot.

of you who ask why a spaceship doesn't land in front of the White House, there is your answer. Don't for one minute think that a spaceship landing on the North Lawn would create a peaceful incident. It would be chaotic and with our quick trigger fingers, there would be death.

Our political, social, and cultural frameworks will probably be shaken if we gain knowledge from an advanced civilization. This is often what change does. It shakes things up. It causes distress. Some will lose fortunes, some will gain fortunes. For the ones who have a tight grip on our economic and political institutions, a change towards a kinder, gentler Earth could cause them to lose what they hold so dear: power and money.

We are not ready for an alien landing. We need to purge and heal many of our societal ills first. I believe we are in the process of that. The current political climate in the U.S. is illuminating the serious problems in our governmental institutions. We also haven't learned to love one another. We are still working on that. Until we accept and love one another, how can we harmoniously interact with an alien civilization? We need to make peace at home first, before extending peace to another civilization. Otherwise, we will inflict upon them the fears and hostilities we inflict upon one another here on Earth.

Right now, we live like the kid whose mom won't let him play with the neighbors. We have chosen to isolate ourselves from the rest of the cosmos. All the reasons for hiding and covering up the truth, I do not know. What I do know is that we are in a reveal. The truth is being divulged in a variety of ways through books and movies and TV shows. There is a momentum gaining intensity and soon, Earthlings will have to acknowledge they share the universe with other intelligent life.

Our lack of planetary peace does not stop aliens or ETs from visiting us. ET stands for extraterrestrial. The Merriam-Webster definition of extraterrestrial is *"originating, existing, or occurring outside the earth or its atmosphere."* Currently, there are two schools of thought regarding ET contact. One is the extraterrestrial hypothesis (ETH) and the other is the interdimensional hypothesis (IDH). Both are attempts to make sense of something which we fully do not understand.

The origins of ETH and IDH are unknown. There have been several scientists, astronomers, and UFOologists referring to these hypotheses for decades.

ETH is based on the belief that ETs are living beings, visiting from another planet. They get into a flying saucer, zip through space, and enter our atmosphere. They walk around and sometimes interact with humans. Sometimes, they don't leave their spaceships but fly around for us to see them. They have technology more advanced than ours, explaining how they zip through space. If we could move through space as quickly as they, we would be able to visit their planets and interact with them too. All of this is predicated on the belief that we and the ETs live in the same dimension.

IDH is based on the belief that ETs are living beings, visiting from other dimensions. They get into a flying saucer, zip through dimensions and enter our reality but not our three dimensional reality. The ETs communicate with us in the dimensions beyond the three we know of. There are more than three dimensions on Earth. According to quantum physics, there are many dimensions and many universes, or multiverses.

A dimension is a level of reality. Humans see in three dimensions, or 3D. The first dimension gives us length, such as a straight line drawn on paper. The second dimension adds height, such as a square drawn on paper. The third dimension adds depth, such as a cube. The Superstring Theory, in quantum physics, postulates there are ten dimensions in the universe. The fourth dimension is time, the fifth dimension is a band from the sixties or where parallel worlds exist, the sixth through tenth dimensions are also planes of reality where other worlds or multiverses exist. I personally believe there are more than ten dimensions. I believe there are an infinite number of dimensions.

You are more than 3D. You exist in multiple dimensions beyond three. Don't believe me? Then point to your mind. You can't. You can point to your brain, but you cannot point to your mind. There is no anatomy book which locates the mind. Point to your soul. You can't. Point to your higher self. You can't. Your mind, soul, and higher self exist in dimensions beyond the first, second, and third. Your 3D self is just a sliver of your whole self.

You cannot see many dimensions because they are composed of energy having frequencies higher than what your eyes can register. This is why you cannot see your mind, soul, and higher self. Just because you can't see them doesn't mean they don't exist. You can't see microwaves, radio waves, and sound waves, but you know they exist.

There is an energy field, or aura, surrounding you. Everything exudes energy, this is scientifically proven. This energy field emits color and sound. You are actually a walking orchestra and light show. You can see the auras of humans and animals. It just takes practice. Your eyes can be trained to see some of the higher frequencies.

The part of you existing in the higher dimensions communicates with beings in the higher dimensions. You have the 3D part of you communicating with 3D beings and you have the '3D plus' parts of you communicating with a different set of beings

Every day, billions of people around the world have interdimensional communication with a being living in another dimension. It is called a prayer. There are different types of prayers. One type is a conversation with a non-human entity such an angel or spirit guide. You cannot see the entity because it does not live on Earth. This being knows everything about you. You believe it can manipulate events to make your prayers come true. This being is all knowing, having more knowledge about the universe than you do. And you trust it whole heartedly. You put your life in its hands. Does this make logical sense? No! Is this type of inter-dimensional communication socially acceptable? Yes!

By definition, any being which does not reside on Earth is an extraterrestrial or ET. Wouldn't that include angels, spirit guides, Hindu gods, and others? If Jesus lives in Heaven, which exists outside of Earth's atmosphere, and you believe him to be a living being, that makes him an ET.

Why does our Western society say it's ok to talk to some otherworldly beings but not to others? If I told a stranger on the street that I had a conversation with an angel this morning, they would not blink twice. If I told the same stranger I talked to an ET this morning, they would think I am crazy. When we stop picking and choosing which ETs are socially acceptable to talk to and which ones aren't, we will end the hypocrisy. And don't forget you, too, are an ET in the eyes of other inter-stellar beings.

Since Earthlings are violent, visiting ETs are safer using the IDH method of interaction. Many people are having ET contact via this method whether they know it or not. Inter-dimensional ET contact is often misinterpreted as dreams or hallucinations, if you even remember them. Most inter-dimensional ET contact is not consciously remembered. The 3D portion of your brain can't compute the multi-dimensional, so it does one of two things. One, the brain may place the event in the subconscious. This is why some experiencers (the term abductee is no longer used) undergo hypnosis. Two, the brain may search for a logical explanation, identifying the event as a dream or hallucination. Logical explanations are not always correct.

Hence, the dilemma of inter-dimensional experiencers: we think we are crazy or making things up. The higher self knows what happened was not a dream. Our gut tells us it was not imaginary. We have a deep knowing that the *dream is real.* However, we cannot logically explain it to ourselves and to others. So, we try to dismiss it. We try to file it away, but the truth cannot be buried. As long as we are stuck on explaining everything in terms of a three dimensional framework, we are not going to understand how ET contact and the universe work.

There are ETs similar to us frequency-wise but are much more advanced. Maybe these ETs are us in the future. It is quite possible that our future selves can go back and forth between the past and the future. There are many kinds of advanced ETs and maybe our future selves are just one type.

The most popular type of ET, due to movies, TV, and books, is the Grey. It is the kind of ET with a big head and large dark eyes, with a tiny nose and mouth. It has two arms and two legs and is much smaller than us in stature. They don't speak aloud with words. They speak telepathically.

The Greys are not the only type of ET. There are documented reports of ETs who look similar to us but taller, some that look like giant bugs, and some who look like a cross between a reptile and a human. How many types of ETs are there? Unlimited amounts. If we try to calculate all the planets and stars in the universe multiplied by all the dimensions, that equates to limitless amounts of possible life forms.

There is a slow reveal going on. Our governments are coming out with the truth about our ET relationships. It is happening in dosages we can handle. The more we, the people, demand a higher dosage, the more we will be given what we need. It all depends on how much we push the leaders of our countries for the truth. We, the people, outnumber all the Presidents, Prime Ministers, billionaires, industry leaders, and media moguls, yet we allow them to determine what universal truths we know and when we know it.

This book is my personal effort to join the global momentum towards truth. I have embarked on the journey of personal authenticity and, lo and behold, ETs came up. I didn't know that was going to happen when I started my path of spiritual awakening. The ET truth was presented to me in a way which I cannot ignore nor completely understand. It freaked me out and confused the hell out of me. The hardest part was hiding it. I tried for many years to ignore my experiences, but what happened to me the second night I moved to Arapahoe, North Carolina, made it impossible for me to keep quiet.

Why am I on this difficult journey of authenticity and spiritual awakening? Because I desire personal peace. I desire it more than anything. My desire for peace makes me look in the dark corners of my mind and shine light on what I have been hiding. The reveal isn't pretty. Identifying the protective layers, or lies, I piled on to shield me from the truth is imperative. I must shed these layers or I cannot fulfill my potential and create a life of fulfillment. What is my potential and the potential of every human? A life of internal peace.

In my quest to fulfill my potential, I cannot smother the authentic version of myself. I yearn to live on a planet which also displays its authentic version of itself. Just as I peel back the lies about myself, I want our society to peel back its lies about itself.

I believe denying the truth about who we are prevents us from finding peace, personally and collectively.

In this book, I present a very fast history of my life as it applies to the struggles of accepting my ET contacts. I share with you some of my supernatural incidents to illustrate the fact that we are multi-dimensional beings living in a multi-dimensional universe. I describe the ET events which dramatically altered my reality and how these events promoted a more powerful and happier version of myself.

There are parts in the book which may seem scary. They were scary to me, at the time. I now have a different perspective and have transcended the debilitating hold fear had on me. In other words, this is a happy alien story.

So, here I am being the most vulnerable I have ever been. I risk ridicule and that has been a fear I have had my entire life. In order for me to be my most authentic self, I need to face this fear and tell my truth. Here it is. Here is my life-long story about me and the aliens.

YOU HAVE THE RIGHT TO TALK TO ALIENS

A PARANORMAL LIFE

As a little girl, my attention is focused on my soul, astral travel, UFOs, meditation, psychic abilities, reincarnation, and the afterlife. My parents do not adhere to a particular religion, despite being raised Muslim in Istanbul, Turkey, where I am born in 1963.

My parents combine the first syllables in their names to create mine. My name, Sever, means *to love*, in Turkish. My last name, Tok, means *full*. In college, I decide to shorten my name to Sev, which also means *to love*, because my full name is difficult for Americans to pronounce.

My parents make the decision to move to America and we leave Istanbul while I am a baby. The first stop is Montreal, Canada where my sister is born. A few years later, we arrive in America and settle down in the Virginia/Washington, D.C. suburbs. My parents barely know English when we arrive. Crofton, Maryland is where we live the longest and where most of my growing up happens.

I admire my parents for leaving all their family, friends, and a comfortable lifestyle to come to America. My father's father, Basri Tok, owned the only distributorship of General Mo-

tors' auto parts in all of Turkey. During my grandfather's lifetime, the Turkish Empire, or Ottoman Empire, was governed by
Sultans. It was one of the largest and richest dynasties in the
world. The Sultans ruled for six hundred years until 1922.
Mustafa Kemal Ataturk founded the Republic of Turkey in 1923.
Ataturk is like the Turkish George Washington, highly admired,
honored, and respected.

My father's mother, a teacher, was the daughter of a high-
ranking officer in the Ottoman Army. My father's parents were
the upper class, so he was afforded a life with travels through
Europe and access to the finest schools.

My mother comes from a notable family too. My mother's
father, Telat Heris, was a Lieutenant Colonel in the Turkish
Army and had a personal working-relationship with the highly
revered Ataturk, who was President of Turkey from 1923 to
1938. Ataturk ushered in a new era of democracy and freedom
from religious dictates.

Despite their upbringing, my parents do not identify with
any organized religion and, as my sister and I mature, do not
push religion on us. They encourage us to investigate and ask
questions about all religions. We are told we can pick any religion to belong; or we can belong to none. Our house is filled
with books about all religions and we are encouraged to read,
ask questions, and mentally explore.

I start first grade not knowing English. The first few years of elementary school, my parents send us to private school. Since English is a foreign language to us, they hope we get the special attention private schools offer. By Christmas, I am conversing with my schoolmates. I am introduced to a strange custom of putting a tree in the house and piling gifts under it. In art class, we are to make a manger with Jesus in it. I have no idea what a manger is and have never heard of Jesus.

"Who is Jesus?" I ask.

I am given a lesson in religion from a group of seven year olds. "Jesus is the son of God," my classmates respond, while they cut construction paper. "And Christmas is his birthday." It does not make sense to me that there is a fat man named Santa Claus who flies through the air with animals, delivering gifts under a tree in the house. Since it seems utterly unrealistic to me, I never believe in Santa Claus. Further proof comes when I see my mother purchase the Christmas toys from Toys "R" Us.

While my sister and I are in elementary school, my parents delve into their spiritual expansion. Many evenings, I sit in the living room with my parents and their American friends, listening to the fascinating conversations contemplating the meaning of life. I learn how to meditate in fifth grade. My meditation room is the walk-in closet. I sit on the floor, in the dark, my eyes closed, concentrating on my third eye. My spiritual awareness begins at an early age.

In the early 70's, we buy bottled water, take vitamins, and eat health food. Many of my parents' friends make fun of our healthy lifestyle and spiritual practices. None of my school friends are meditating or contemplating the purpose of life, so I don't talk about it. I learn at a very young age to hide the truth about myself.

My father plays psychic games with us as we grow up. We try to guess what number he is thinking. We try to guess the geometric shape he draws on a piece of paper. We bend spoons a la Uri Geller. We make small pinwheels spin without touching them, using only the energy emitted from our hands. My sister and I share with my parents what we see and hear in our meditations. My reality, as a child, includes the knowledge that we emit energy, there are many dimensions, and there is more to the human body than what our eyes see. As a family, we believe there is life on other planets too.

Shortly after my father's death in 2016, my mother hands me a black and white composition book. In it are his handwritten descriptions of his supernatural experiences which began as a child in Istanbul. He never mentions this book to me, so it comes as a surprise when my mother gives it to me. My mother also gives me his camera, for he was a professional photographer. Between the camera and the book, I feel I have a tangible connection to my father's heart and soul.

Like my father, I also have supernatural experiences as a child. I consciously travel between dimensions without understanding what is happening. I tell myself these are all intense, life-like dreams and keep them to myself. I don't tell my parents about my visits from my galactic friend, either. Why? I don't know. One would think the open-minded atmosphere my parents create for us would encourage me to tell them. My entire childhood I feel as if I am an observer on Earth, meant to keep quiet and to just watch.

One school morning, as I lay in bed awake, I cannot open my eyes. I can feel the pillow, my hands under my pillow, and the bed. All of a sudden, I see very clearly a cowboy getting shot and rolling in the dust. The next thing I know, I am flying through the air in spirit form. My legs are gone and feel like sheets flapping in the wind. I am flying through space. Then golden eyes on a black cat appear and move slowly towards me, the golden eyes getting bigger and bigger. I still cannot open my eyes. My mother opens our bedroom door and says, in Turkish, "It's time to get ready for school!" My mother's voice chases away the cat and pops my eyes open. I get out of bed and get ready to go to sixth grade. I tell no one about this experience.

I wonder about it for the next thirty-eight years, until I see those large, golden cat eyes again.

In junior high, I realize I know things about people I cannot normally know. My attempts to share with my friends what I think is obvious information, is met with "How do you know that? You can't know that!" So, I learn to shut up and keep it all to myself.

I live in two worlds. The outside world where I try my best to be very normal and my world at home, where my sister and I are encouraged to expand our minds, think outside the box, and be abnormal.

I am thirteen when the first Star Wars movie is released. My father and I are blown away. One year later, Battlestar Galactica premiers on TV. My father and I wait for its debut with excitement. It is around this time I begin to do automatic writing. I hold a pen to paper, calm my mind, and as information enters my head, I write it all down. I tell no one about the writings. Now, automatic writing is called channeling.

While in high school, my father comes home from work with a gift for us. It is a Ouija board. We are all fascinated. We play with it as a family and individually. One evening, my mother's girlfriend comes over and wants to experience the Ouija board. She and I sit on the floor, at the coffee table, and put our hands on the planchette. My parents sit on the couch, watching us. Our hands start to move. The letters spell out something I do not understand at all. It is gibberish to me.

My mother announces that her father is in the room. He died many years prior. "Rol yapma," she says in Turkish because the Ouija board spells it out. Literally translated it means *don't play a role*. In other words, don't fake it or don't put on a show. My grandfather would say this to my mother when she was little, but I do not know this as our hands slide over the board. My mother's friend is American and knows no Turkish. We are all astonished by my mother's announcement that her dead father just spoke with us.

This fascination with the paranormal starts to wane as I enter college. I am focused on earning a biology degree from Loyola College (now Loyola University) in Baltimore. It is ironic I attend a Catholic school. I don't engage in any Catholic-related activities. I am there for an excellent education. My intention is to go to medical school.

I live on campus in college. One morning, my roommate says to me, "Sev. I don't want to scare you, but when I walked into our bedroom last night while you were sleeping, there was a bright beam of light shining directly on you from outside the window. It was not from a street lamp. It was eerie and weird. Does this scare you?"

"No," I reply and don't think twice about it.

Many times during high school and as a young adult, I feel my bed shake while I am in a light sleep. I feel things touching me which I cannot see. It doesn't scare me though.

In my junior year of college, I have an internship at a local hospital. It makes me change my mind about medical school. I earn my Bachelor of Science degree in Biology in 1985 and toy with the idea of studying acupuncture. I pick an acupuncturist out of the phone book and call him, wondering if I may ask him some questions. He talks me out of studying acupuncture, claiming it is not easy to make a living since the majority of Americans do not accept it as a valid form of healing.

After graduating college, I am not sure what to do since I decide not to go to medical school or acupuncture school. I have no desire to use my biology degree, either. I get a job making jewelry for a designer. I have a very creative, artistic side which is important for me to express. I enjoy this job. I then start my own wholesale jewelry-design business with sales reps around the country. I am in my early twenties and living at home. It is successful quickly, but due to some family issues, I decide to shut it down and go to Turkey. I intend on visiting for a month, but stay for six months.

Shortly after returning to the U.S., I meet my husband. I get married for the first time when I am in my late twenties. His abusive tendencies are apparent from the start, but I am too naive and inexperienced to recognize them.

During the marriage, my paranormal abilities begin to intensify. One summer afternoon while I sit in the sun on the deck, with my eyes closed, a face appears and tells me his name. It startles me so much that my eyes pop open and I bolt out of my chair. I hear a voice tell me to look in the obituary section of the newspaper. I walk to the newspaper, telling myself I am crazy. There, in the obituary section, is his name. He has just died. I am shocked.

My husband comes home and I tell him what happened. All he says is, "Don't read the obituaries." His response is so dismissive and unsupportive, that I decide to never tell him about my supernatural experiences again. I don't share with him the dream I have of an airplane flying through a tall, glass building by the water. Four years later, on September 11, I see the same image on TV.

I re-start my jewelry business. This time I concentrate on retail and sell my jewelry on kiosks in the major malls around Baltimore. I start to channel again and write volumes about spiritual concepts. The information coming forth is not from me. It is knowledge I do not know. It is all very beautiful about the purpose of life and how love is the basis of all creation. I write and write and get much pleasure from the serenity of the messages.

I start the roller coaster. I channel and write page after page. I think I'm crazy and throw all the pages away. I tell myself never to channel again, but I can't stay away from it. I start again. I write, tell myself I'm crazy, and throw it all away. I do this numerous times. I feel like I am losing my mind.

Dead people won't leave me alone. I see them while I am awake and while I sleep. They tell me about their lives and have messages for their families. I don't do anything with the information. I insist they all go away. It isn't until a few years later I learn how to control these visits. I teach myself how to control the flow of inter-dimensional information so it doesn't have to be all or nothing. "They" don't have control over me. I can set the rules for their visits so that my life and sleep are not interrupted.

During my marriage, my best friend dates a writer. He gets a job writing a short story for Star Wars. He tells me, "Sev Tok. I like your name. I am going to name a planet after you." I laugh and don't take him seriously. Sure enough, in *Star Wars Adventure Journal 9,* the short story *Droids Defiant* written by Tom Bowling includes the Sev Tok star system. It contains the planet Sev Tok with two moons. As a young girl, watching the first Star Wars movie, I never imagine there will be a star system and planet named after me in the Star Wars galactic system. I am in Wookieepedia too.

When my marriage ends due to verbal and physical abuse, I close the jewelry business. I become a floral designer for a chain of florist shops and am promoted to territory manager. I live with my parents and then my sister's family for a few months and get laid off. I become a manufacturer's rep for an internationally known tool company, calling on the the big home improvement stores. I rent a rowhouse in the Fells Point section of Baltimore City and meet my next husband.

I grow to dislike my job, so I quit. I become a manufacturer's rep for a home goods company, calling on the largest retailers in the U.S. My life is filled with lots of jobs because I am never fulfilled with any of them. Because I go from job to job, I wonder if there is something wrong with me. It seems like everyone else has a career and is stable, except me. I just can't seem to find the right career. My first job, as a teenager, is a lifeguard. From there, I have so many different jobs, I cannot even remember all of them.

My second marriage makes me happy for several years. We have a good life. We have a nice home by the water, in the Canton section of Baltimore City. We have the boat, the cars, the vacations, the dinner parties, the everything that looks beautiful from the outside.

Once again, I grow to dislike my job and quit. I start my jewelry business again. I go to big and small art festivals around Maryland and success comes quickly. I decide to open a retail store in the Harborplace in Baltimore's Inner Harbor. Soon, I end my jewelry business due to lack of enjoyment. What was a fun hobby turns into stressful work which takes over my life. I have no idea what to do next. An unexpected job offer comes from the CPA firm where my sister works. I begin my new job thinking it is temporary and wind up staying there for several years.

I begin to channel again. I am now forty-five years old and I am at a crossroads. I need to know if I am crazy or not. If I am crazy, I will get help. If I am not, then I will do something with my paranormal abilities.

Without me asking, three people tell me about a psychic in Baltimore. I take this as a sign. She is the one who will give me my answer. I make an appointment with her. I am skeptical. Even though I know channeling is a genuine process, she has to prove herself to me.

I go to the psychic, something that is actually very unusual for me to do. I sit down and she asks me what my question is. I don't want to lead her on, so I don't tell the truth. I tell her I have no question and to tell me what I need to know. She tells me that everyone has a question. I insist I do not.

She closes her eyes and right away she says, "You can see and hear very well. You should be doing what I am doing." I am relieved. She continues for half an hour. I leave feeling energized and happy that I am not bonkers.

By the time I get home after a thirty minute drive, I tell myself, "Poor thing. She is just as crazy as I am." I struggle with believing her. As much as I try to dismiss what she says, I cannot stop thinking about it. Two months later, I call a friend and ask her to send me a stranger to "read." She calls me back and says she has two ladies who want to come over at the same time.

"Two? What are you doing to me?! I don't even know if I can do one!" I think to myself.

Instead of expressing my fear, I politely say, "Thank you." I am the most nervous I have ever been. I am either going to look like a fool or I am going to fly. The little devil on my shoulder reminds me that I can cancel. The little angel on my other shoulder reminds me of having regrets on my deathbed. I don't want to wonder, for the rest of my life, if I really have psychic abilities. As I wait for the ladies, I almost vomit from the nerves.

They arrive. The readings go well. I can do it! Whew! My second husband encourages me to explore my abilities. When I tell him I want to have people over so I can read them, he is supportive. I conduct the readings on the weekends, at home, while working at the accounting firm full time.

I do the readings for free at first. Pretty soon, I get so busy, I begin to charge a fee and look for office space. The owner of a successful acupuncture clinic in Hampden, a hipster section of Baltimore City, offers me space on Sundays. She gives me the opportunity to go legit. I am on cloud nine and very thankful for her.

On New Year's Eve 2012, I leave my second husband because his actions and words push me beyond my limits. I spend the first day of the new year in my parents' bed crying all day. I am heart-broken. I feel alone and, at the age of forty-eight, have to create a whole new life for myself.

I harbor no anger or resentment towards my ex-husbands. It was completely my choice to accept their behavior. I take full responsibility for the bad and the good in my life. I played the victim well, but I don't play that role anymore.

After leaving my second marriage, I embark on my spiritual path. I work very hard to eliminate the victim vibe from my personal energy. I succeed in erasing this inhibitive thought pattern and my life changes for the better. For the first time, I feel in control and powerful. I create a fulfilling career and have an active, enjoyable life.

I share my life of many jobs and two husbands to illustrate how frustrating life can be when you ignore your heart's messages. Personal relationships suffer. Careers suffer. If we can instill in our children and young adults the importance of being authentic, how different our western society could be.

Trying to appease parents or others is a sure fire way to destroy your personal spark. I denied my psychic abilities and tried to fit into jobs that were safe and "normal." What I really wanted to do was to explore spirituality and my psychic abilities. I don't know what kind of job I could have had, but if I simply followed that path, I know I would have found jobs better suited to my nature.

When I embark on my spiritual journey, the alien contact increases; or maybe the contact has always been there, but I become more aware of it. This does not mean you will be abducted by aliens if you embark on your spiritual journey. The aliens are part of *my* journey, not necessarily yours.

The supernatural and alien experiences I share with you are not to brag or to imply that I am special. My intent is to help anyone who has similar experiences. There are many of you who do. If there was a book like this years ago, it would have helped me a great deal. So, I am writing the book I wish I read.

I also want to emphasize that we all have paranormal abilities. I don't care for the word paranormal because it implies out of the normal, not ordinary. ESP, clairvoyance, speaking with the dead, talking to ETs, seeing auras, etc. are normal abilities. What is abnormal is denying it.

Sensitivity to messages from the multi-dimensions is not a curse. It makes me sad when someone thinks they are disadvantaged for having heightened paranormal abilities. Using your psychic abilities is advantageous. It is like having a leg up on life. Your supernatural abilities are free tools for you to use to make your life easier, not harder. I encourage you to strengthen your abilities in order to help others and to help yourself manifest your life to your standards.

RAMPED UP

I live alone for four years after ending my second marriage. My best girlfriends in Baltimore and Maui are absolutely invaluable to me during my single years. I rely on these ladies for my self-preservation and they do a terrific job in making sure I am mentally, physically, and spiritually all right.

I stay single for four years because I am on a quest for self-discovery. I date a lot. I date men much younger than I and men who are my own age. I give myself freedom to be, with no interest in others' opinions about how to live my life. I have a lot of fun.

Along with the fun is the not-so-much-fun part of deep personal exploration. The journey of spiritual awakening is a trip into the hidden, secret places within me. I need to know why I married two men who exhibit abusive behaviors. I have to figure it out because I just cannot not do that again. I do not want my next relationship to be with the same type of man.

Since everything is made up of energy and radiates its energy, you align with people, places, and events which have a similar energy to yours. I call it the Law of Alignment. To me, the popular Law of Attraction means you have to attract something, as if you have to suck it from across the room.

Quantum physics says the energy of everything is simultaneously everywhere. So, the energy of what you want is hovering right in front of you. There is nothing to attract. All you have to do is align with it by radiating a similar frequency. Everyone and every situation in your life is there because it has an energy similar to yours. Want to make a change? Change your vibe.

Making the vibratory shift involves deep self-introspection which is not for the weak of heart. Such work is for the brave and courageous. You have to identify beliefs and patterns in your life which are hard to accept. The ego has to be pushed out the window.

After leaving my second marriage, I move into an apartment in a trendy and historic part of Baltimore City. It is a stylish loft apartment located down a hill, amongst trees, in a secluded area. There are businesses, artist studios, and a popular restaurant in the complex, but it still feels like I am tucked away from the rest of the city. It is here that I do the bulk of my self-introspection and self-discovery. And it is also here that I become very aware of ET activity. It feels as if the ETs are ramping up their contact with me. I try to brush off the many marks on my body, strange lights, and unshakable memories. Some of it I share with my girlfriends, some of it I do not.

The very first night in my new apartment, it is just me and Napoleon, my little rescue dog. We snuggle with each other trying to fit in the tiny cot, the only piece of furniture in the apartment. Even though I don't have much tangibly, I am rich with freedom. I go to sleep that first night with a smile on my face.

Shortly before I return Napoleon to my ex-husband, I have a dream. In it, I pick up a black kitten that has light beams coming out of its eyes. It has one white hair on its paw, one on its back, and another one on its chest. I ask someone in the dream if the kitten belongs to anyone and she tells me it doesn't. I say, "I am taking it home." Upon awakening, I know my black cat is on its way. Since the "dream" in sixth grade, when those golden cat eyes approached me, I have always known I will have a black cat one day and its name will be Zulu.

I tell my girlfriend, Randi, about my dream and that my black cat is on its way. The very next day, she calls me and says she is at the plant nursery and there is a kitten there. Someone at the nursery is finding homes for a litter of kittens and there is just one left.

"Is it black?" I inquire.

"Yes."

"It's mine. Please take it home and I will come and get it." I say matter-of-factly. When I get to Randi's house and see the kitten, I recognize she is the one in my dream. She has the same white hairs on her paw, back, and chest. I know this kitten is very special and will be an Earthly spirit guide for me.

Shortly after bringing Zulu home, she tells me who she is. One morning, I awaken abruptly. My eyes pop open quickly. In my face are large, golden cat eyes on a black face. Zulu is sitting so close to my face, staring at me while I sleep, that when I open my eyes, her face is all I see. I am startled and immediately re-member those same eyes from sixth grade. She has been with me for a long time. Not only in this lifetime but in others. We form a very tight bond. She is energetically plugged into me in a very strong way.

My other black cat, Comet, also comes to me in a unique fashion. I see her in spirit form before she actually appears in her 3D body. I clearly see her ghost in the doorway of my bed-room. I tell Randi that I think I am getting another black cat. Once again, Randi plays matchmaker. She calls me from the vet saying a black kitten needs a home. Before I go to the vet to get the kitten, I think about what to name her. I hear in my head that it should be a space-related name. I decide on Comet.

When I arrive at the vet, I see a flyer pinned to the bul-letin board with pictures of the kittens from the litter. The back-ground is space-themed and each kitten has a space name. They give my kitten the name Aurora. Since she has a little white spot on her chest resembling a comet, I stick with the name Comet. And her favorite place to sleep is in the doorway of my bedroom.

I have many inter-dimensional kitty stories. It is natural for animals to communicate like this. Often, humans don't listen to the messages our pets send us. Not only do they talk to us while we are awake, they talk to us while we sleep.

One night in my dream, I see Zulu stuck in a closet. I awaken, call out her name and she does not come. I get out of bed and climb down the stairs. I know which closet to walk to and open the door. She runs and out with a disgruntled meow.

How does she communicate with me while I sleep? She is awake in the closet yet taps into me while I am dreaming. How does she do that?! I do not know. Humans, animals, and ETs communicate in ways which science cannot yet explain.

One year after moving into my stylish apartment, I quit my accounting job and start my own business. Finally, at the age of 49, I have a fulfilling career doing spiritual readings. Because my new business is in its early stages of growth, I struggle with paying the rent. I move to a less expensive place close by. This time I rent the top floor of a lovely Victorian home in Roland Park, an upscale neighborhood in Baltimore City.

The ET contact continues. Often, I have strange marks on my body. Sometimes, the marks are geometric. I laugh to myself how funny it is that a bug would bite me in the shape of a perfect triangle. One time, I look at my arm to see a half inch indentation. It looks like someone took a scoop out of my skin. It is small but deep. There is no blood, not even a scab. It is very clean and I wonder how it happened, where is the blood, and how did I not feel it?

Many times, I wake up without any clothes on. I go to bed clothed and awake naked. I wake up to loud bangs which I cannot explain. I get out of bed and look around for something that may have fallen and find nothing. One evening, my eyes open in the middle of the night and there is a bright light in the hallway. I tell myself I left a light on, knowing there is no light that would shine that brightly into the hallway. When I get up in the morning, all the lights are off.

I experience sleep paralysis often. I feel something in the bedroom with me and I cannot move. I feel a presence laying beside me or pressing against me. I can feel it touching me. When this happens to me as a teenager and young adult, it does not scare me. Now, as a mature adult, it scares me. I never insist the presence go away. I am under the false belief that it has control over me. I learn later that I am the one who always has the power, not "them."

Shortly after moving into the Victorian house, I meet the gentleman who rents the second floor, beneath my floor. Within minutes, he tells me he is going to a UFO Conference in a few days and that he is chipped by aliens. They monitor him. I am surprised he says this to me, a perfect stranger to him. He has no idea that I am a believer in aliens. I also find it amazing that out of all the apartments I can move to, I pick one where my downstairs neighbor believes ETs are tracking him.

During my single years, as I delve into my spiritual awakening, my psychic abilities strengthen. After all, the business I start is all about the paranormal. I create a business where I do intuitive readings. In the beginning, I call myself a Medium and then decide I don't like the word. I begin to call myself a Soul Purpose Coach because I conduct Soul Purpose Readings.

The information I channel provides enlightenment and clarity for my clients. What is divulged in a Soul Purpose Reading is why you are here, what your purpose is, and how to fulfill it. A past life is usually described which clarifies an issue in the current life. Belief systems inhibiting you from achieving success in various areas of your life are identified. We discuss how to alleviate these negative beliefs to allow for personal enrichment and satisfaction. I help my clients achieve personal peace by conscious creation. We talk about the energy human beings radiate and how that energy creates one's reality. I basically help people become as happy as possible.

What or who am I channeling during a reading? I can hear, feel and see information from my client's energy field, spirit guides, the dead, and entities living in other dimensions. I also "download" information from the matrix of energy floating around us, known as Earth's Collective Consciousness. In this energetic matrix floats information about people, beliefs, and attitudes of our planet.

Before a client comes for their reading, all I want to know about them is their first name. I do not want to know anything else about them. When they arrive, the reading starts right away. I don't even want to make chit chat. The purpose for this is validation. If I know nothing about them, and if the information presented in the reading is accurate and true, then my client trusts the process.

As I write this, I have been doing Soul Purpose Readings for eight years and I have conducted thousands of them. Many of my clients get multiple readings through the years. This is the most fulfilled I have ever been in terms of my career and personal life. I am over joyed with my personal successes. It was tough to get to this point but very well worth the struggle, tears, and occasional bouts of self-doubt.

Anyone can get information from spirit guides, the dead, inter-dimensional entities, and Earth's Collective Consciousness. All you have to do is three things. First, believe that such information exists. Second know that you can hear, feel, and see inter-dimensional information. Third, practice, practice, practice.

You strengthen your inter-dimensional muscles by practicing through meditation. You can get to the point where you have a clear channel 24/7, so you can hear, feel, and see without needing to meditate. It becomes second nature. When you become this connected to the multi-dimensions, life becomes easier. Why? Because you receive helpful guidance from the higher perspective which is a very valuable viewpoint from which to make decisions about your life.

Psychic information comes in the form of intuition, gut feelings, hunches, dreams, and visions. We are all multi-dimensional beings with psychic abilities. There is nothing special about me. I have just been exercising my paranormal muscles since childhood.

YOU HAVE THE RIGHT TO TALK TO ALIENS

HYBRID REUNION

2013, Baltimore, Maryland

They are the bluest eyes I have ever seen. They are wide open and not focused on anything. I stare at the face, then the body, then the liquid around the body, and then the tube. I know it is a boy even though I cannot see any genitals due to the placement of its legs. I am standing in front of a large glass tube, taller than I am and about as wide. There is a baby floating in the tube. I look behind the tube and see nothing, for I and the baby are in a very dark room.

I look over my right shoulder and standing several feet behind me, in the darkness, are three Greys. One is tall, the other medium in height, and the third the shortest. Telepathically, they tell me they are giving me my space. They are giving me personal time with the baby. They are kind and do not scare me at all. They don't rush me and are patient, telling me to take my time.

I turn back to the baby in the tube very confused. Why are they giving me time with this baby? I have no maternal instincts towards it. Who is this baby? Why is it in a tube? I feel very neutral towards it. I feel more emotion when I look at a

41

bouquet of flowers.

My eyes pop open. There is no grogginess. It is an instant state of awake. I am in my bed. I lie there for a while absorbing what I saw because I am also having a physical reaction to it. *That was real.*

At this time, I do not know much about hybridization efforts with humans and ETs. I do not know that Greys come in different heights. I also think that the Greys are cold and emotionless, but these Greys are sympathetic and warm.

When I entertain the possibility that the baby is mine, I halt the thought. It freaks me out. Deep, deep, very deep inside, I know the baby has my DNA. What a secret to carry. When people ask me if I have children, I want to reply, "Yes, but not human children." For years, I tell no one about it.

DRAWING OF BABY IN TUBE

YOU HAVE THE RIGHT TO TALK TO ALIENS

HELP

Toward the end of the lease in my Victorian apartment, I want to leave Baltimore and know I am finished with dating. One afternoon, while sitting on my bedroom floor sorting laundry, I stare up to the ceiling and loudly declare "I am done! I am ready for a serious relationship. I will accept no other reality. And I need to have a boat in my life again." I owned a boat in my previous marriage and missed boating very much. I am the happiest when I am on the water.

A few mornings later, I arise from bed to feed the cats and a very loud voice, in my head, tells me to sign up on an internet dating sight. This is something I refuse to do while single. Many times, my friends recommend I go on a dating site and the thought of it feels like a knife stabbing me in the stomach. So when this voice announces itself, I argue with it. I battle with it. Finally, it wins.

I go to the computer reluctantly. Which dating site do I use? I settle on a very popular one and start the endless questionnaire. I have a brand new computer with no pictures of myself. I take a picture with the computer camera of me sitting at the keyboard. It comes time to pay for the site and the shortest term is six months. "No way!" I exclaim to myself. I really just want to do this for one day, to appease this voice.

I find another sight which I have barely heard of. Again, I go through the questionnaire and put one picture of me sitting at the keyboard. The payment plan is for three months and that is much better than six. With all of that out of the way, I leave to visit my parents for Easter. The voice leaves me alone.

In two weeks, I meet Patrick who has just joined the site. Before we meet, over the phone, Patrick tells me he recently decided to become more spiritual, not really knowing what that means. He lives on Capitol Hill in Washington, D.C. and drives to Baltimore to meet me for dinner. During dinner, he tells me he has a sailboat and draws on a napkin diagrams of how to tack. A couple of months later, we fall in love. I and my two cats leave Baltimore and move in with him.

I do not tell Patrick about my ET travels when we meet. I don't tell him because I don't want him to think I am a kook. Little do I know that soon, my ET contact will become a significant part of our lives.

When all of this ET stuff bursts open, Patrick provides a safe space for me to share my feelings and details about the ETs. He does not judge me nor dismiss me. His nurturing, kind, and accepting responses to my weirdo stories are exactly what I need in order to process and heal.

My girlfriends also provide a nurturing forum for me. I have a spiritually-based career and have cultivated a group of friends who have the same belief system I do. They don't find my ET details weird or crazy. There are experiencers who do not have such an open-minded support system. There are experiencers who have very logic-based professions, whose peer groups are logical thinkers. Logic needs to be swept aside when it comes to ET contact. Logic is a three dimensional form of thought and ET contact is a multi-dimensional event. We need to let go of the need to logically explain things in order to believe in them.

Even though my girlfriends provide much help to me, they are not in the nitty-gritty of it every day like Patrick is. Having a group of people outside the home to confide in is valuable, but having a trusting confidant at home is life-saving.

One of my best girlfriends, MahaDevi, is exceptionally helpful to me. She is a spiritual teacher in Virginia and has had ET contact, herself. With her, I go into detail about my experiences. I also open up completely to her regarding my emotions. Since she is knowledgeable about ETs, is spiritually awakened, and has a very nurturing demeanor, she provides much needed guidance for me. She is available whenever I want to talk and that is often. I call her my "ET therapist."

If you have an inkling that you are involved in ET contact, find someone to talk to. It may be hard, at first, to admit this is happening. If your imaginations and dreams are so dramatic and life-like that you cannot shake them, that is a sign of possible ET contact. Listen to your instincts. Even if you don't have proof of your contact, that does not mean it isn't happening.

CONFERENCE WITH THE GREYS

November 4, 2016, Roswell, New Mexico

When Patrick announces his early retirement, his management comes up with a way to coax him to stay. He is offered a ten-month job on the island of Kauai, in Hawaii, to manage a test program for the U.S. Navy's latest radar system. All expenses paid. Then, he can retire. Not a bad way to spend the last year of a thirty-five year career. I am thrilled, for Hawaii is a very special place for me. My heart sits in Hawaii. I love Hawaii. I spend the ten months traveling between Kauai, Maui, Oahu, and Capitol Hill.

Shortly after Patrick goes to Hawaii to assume his new position, an ET-themed trail begins to form. I become Facebook friends with a gentleman who is very knowledgeable about UFOs. I don't know him, but we have many mutual friends, so I accept his friend request. We talk about UFO-related matters. Right after that, one of my friends, Elizabeth, who lives on Maui, asks me if I know about Corey Goode. I do not. I watch a few videos about him. Then, out of the blue, Patrick tells me he has to go to White Sands Missile Range in New Mexico for work. I am in our townhouse on Capitol Hill when he suggests I meet him in El Paso. He plans a four-day get-a-way for us. He maps out our drive to White Sands and then to Roswell to spend the night. Roswell! He knows that excites me. I have been interested in the UFO crash in Roswell since I was a little girl.

The synchronicity does not escape my attention. I know *something* is going to happen in Roswell. As I enter this trip in my calendar, I draw a giant alien convinced that unknown forces are leading us to an out-of-this world experience.

I have never been to New Mexico before. The scenery is spectacular. I feel as if I am not on Earth. The landscape is beautiful and spooky to me. As we approach White Sands Missile Range, all the hairs on the back of my neck stand up. I get a dark, nefarious feeling. I am very uncomfortable. The Range is located at the base of a black mountain. As Patrick drives closer, I wish he would turn the car around. He has been to the Range a few times over the course of his career and is eager to show it to me. I just want to run in the opposite direction.

He parks the car and I don't want to get out, but I do. I follow him to the museum which has a missile park. It displays the rockets and missiles tested at the Range. As we walk through the park, I find it visually interesting because of all the long and pointy missiles standing side by side. Then I see something which appears misplaced. It looks like a small space ship. I walk up to it and read the plaque beside it. It is the Aeroshell "Flying Saucer" which is a section of the Voyager Balloon System. It was launched near Roswell in 1966. I find it very odd that it is the only thing in the whole park that looks like a space ship. It raises suspicion in my mind.

We go to the museum building and I walk through it as fast as I can. I don't want to rush Patrick, but I want to get the hell out of there. I am hoping that my disinterest in the museum will be noticed, so he doesn't dilly dally. Finally, he is ready to go and I bolt out of the building. As we drive out of the missile range, I tell Patrick I never want to go back there again.

Next we head to the White Sands National Monument to slide down the dunes on sleds. That is a lot of fun. The sand is actually tiny bits of gypsum deposited on a large sea floor millions of years ago. The sea dried up and left this spectacular, white panorama. Once again, the topography looks like another planet. It is beautiful yet strange.

After sledding, we are ready to drive to Roswell. It is a small town and has the International UFO Museum and Research Center. We enjoy the exhibits and the information presented about the Roswell crash. We buy a bunch of alien stuff at the gift shop and then make our way to our hotel close by.

We are both tired. I sit on the bed and turn on the TV. Patrick goes to the bathroom. As I flip through the channels, I silently wish the TV series *People of Earth* would come on so Patrick can watch it. I like that show and he hasn't seen it. Produced by Conan O'Brien, it is a clever and funny take on a support group for alien experiencers. The second season ended a few weeks ago, so I don't think it is on TV anymore.

I stop flipping the channels as Patrick comes out of the bathroom and the screen lands on a commercial. Then, all of a sudden, presto! *People of Earth* appears on the TV. I am stunned. I get a slightly eerie feeling. We watch it, Patrick likes it, we turn off the lights, and fall asleep.

My eyes pop open. It is pitch black in the room. I hear footsteps on the carpet. I feel Patrick climb into the bed. "Why was Patrick sitting on the couch? Was it because of the aliens?" I wonder to myself and fall asleep.

I slowly awaken, in the morning, to the sounds of Patrick in the shower. In my mind, I am trying to make sense of what I heard and felt and knew in the middle of the night. Why would I think Patrick was sitting on the couch? He has never gotten up in the middle of the night to sit on the couch. And why would I think it had to do with aliens? Then, in my mind's eye, I see myself sitting at a table with Greys. We are talking about a book I am writing. The Greys are not mean nor are they nice. They are very neutral. The conference is not a scary experience. I do not remember what is said, but I know it is about a book I am writing.

I sit up in the bed. Patrick is still showering. Like a rush, images and facts gush forward in my mind. All of a sudden I know Greys are creating babies with ET and human DNA. I possess information about human and alien hybridization. I have knowledge I have never known before. I know that the human element the Greys are interested in capturing is emotion. The Grey's population is dying because they don't exercise empathy. They realize compassion is key to keeping a race of people or race of aliens flourishing. I am also knowing that something happened last night while we slept.

Patrick emerges freshly showered. I am still sitting on the bed. The inquisition starts. "Patrick, did you get up in the middle of the night?" I ask, as if I am a court room attorney building a case.

"Yes."

"Did you sit on the couch?" I ask.

"Yes."

My head is swirling. "Why?"

This is where I watch my logical boyfriend struggle. "I know this is going to sound strange. I have never had this feeling before. Something was in the room watching us. I kept looking around and saw nothing. I would try to go back to sleep, but it was intense. Eventually, I had to get out of the bed and sit on the couch."

I just stare at him. "You were tossing and turning on the bed," he continues. "So much so, that I thought you were awake."

He has my attention. If logical Patrick admits to some really strange stuff happening, then it happened. It is not my imagination. We had some kind of ET experience together last night. I cannot piece it all together. I can remember bits of it but not all of it.

This messes with our heads. We are both not feeling right as we continue our vacation. My hands are sweaty and stay sweaty. We both keep staring at the skies expecting to see a saucer as we drive the desolate highways of New Mexico. I tell myself I will feel better when I get back to Capitol Hill.

I don't feel better in Capitol Hill. In fact, I feel worse. I am confused as to why I am talking to Greys about my book. I don't want anything to do with them. I don't want my clients to know about my connection to them. I don't want to be known as the woman who talks to Greys. The book I am writing deals with cultivating self-love to create and manifest the life you desire. There is no room for Greys in it.

I have been afraid of Greys since childhood, with no rational explanation. Because of my fear, I have never read a book about UFOs, Greys, or abductions. Little do I know, that my fear is about to be catapulted off the charts very soon.

Once again, I try to push all of this to the back of mind and continue with my life as if it never happened. The back of my mind is getting pretty full. Soon, I will need to bring the memories to the forefront of my consciousness and demand answers.

YOU HAVE THE RIGHT TO TALK TO ALIENS

SLICED

January 12, 2017, Capitol Hill, Washington, D.C.

Patrick is home for ten days. It is rare for him to be home from Hawaii and I am happy our little family is together. Our little family being the two of us and my two cats.

One morning, as we sit on the couch drinking coffee and watching the news, Patrick says, "What happened to your back?"

"What do you mean?" I inquire. My shirt has lifted on my back and he sees a red, bleeding mark. He grabs his phone and takes a picture. To me, it is plain as day.

"Oh my god! Doesn't it look like a rectangle was sliced out of my back?!" I ask him, incredulous. I see four straight cuts, as if a knife sliced me.

"I guess," he nonchalantly answers. His reaction makes me second guess my assessment. I stare at the half-inch rectangular hole in my skin and begin making excuses for what may have happened. Maybe the cat got me. Maybe I bumped into something, but wouldn't I feel a chunk of skin ripped out of my back? Once again, as I have done my entire life, I try to explain something inexplicable and file it away in the back of my mind.

YOU HAVE THE RIGHT TO TALK TO ALIENS

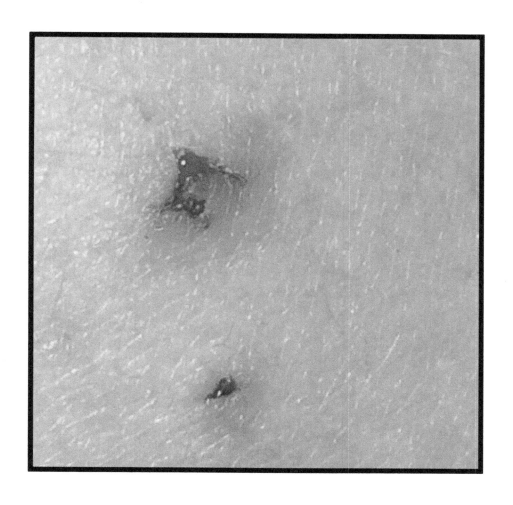

RECTANGLE ON BACK

YOU HAVE THE RIGHT TO TALK TO ALIENS

THE MISSION

Ten months go by since the Roswell incident and I am still not myself. I feel unsettled and the memories of that night interrupt my daily thoughts. I feel as if I have fallen "off track" with my purpose for this lifetime. During these months, I go about my life flying back and forth to Hawaii, conducting Soul Purpose Readings with my clients, holding workshops, speaking on my podcast, writing, and creating videos about spiritual expansion and manifestation. I finally reach the breaking point where it is imperative I know what happened in Roswell and what role I have in all of these ET-related experiences.

Am I supposed to do something with the knowledge I have gained? Am I supposed to "come out" and tell the world? My biggest fear is to be perceived as a screwball or a wacko if I tell others. I reach out to one of my friends for support. She suggests I contact her friend, Dianne Kensler, who is a Master Hypnotist in Virginia, experienced in alien abductions.

Dianne is a three hour car ride, one way. I make an appointment and tell Patrick we are driving to Luray, Virginia so I can be hypnotized. He says, "Okay."

The day of my hypnosis is exactly one year to the day my father passed away. This is interesting to me because my father was a believer in ETs, loved science fiction movies and novels, and was very knowledgeable about space. In fact, he spent his life writing his theory of gravity and astro-physics. When he asked me to help him put his theory in a blog, I was visiting him in his hospital room. I knew once his theory was published on the internet, he would be finished with Earth. It was bittersweet for me to agree to help him. His blog is *Real Universe by Ergun Tok*. I look at it every now and then to feel my father's presence and reminisce. It is appropriate I connect with aliens on the anniversary of my father's departure from Earth.

On the drive to Luray, Virginia, my mind turns back to when I was a little girl. I remember my parents taking me and my sister to Luray Caverns. I describe my memories to Patrick and he wants to see the Caverns too. We decide to visit them after my hypnosis session. I wonder what my state of mind will be afterwards. Will I want to be under the Earth in a cave? Maybe I will want to go straight home. I stare out the windshield not knowing what is going to happen within the next few hours. Whatever happens, I trust it will be exactly what I need.

I ask Patrick to attend my session. I want him there. I want his perspective, his opinions, and if I forget what happens in the session, I need his report. He agrees. I like having him as my witness due to his logical viewpoint and that he does not know much about hypnosis or ETs.

As we arrive to Dianne's office, my heart starts to beat faster. I am anxious. We are a few minutes early, so we sit in the car and I calm myself down by doing a quick meditation. I see a star in my mind's eye. I hear the words "Eternal star. Multi-dimensional fractal star. Star goes into infinity." I understand that the star continues into infinity with each of its limitless, tiniest parts a reflection of the whole. I draw a picture of it. I know what a fractal is and I understand the concept of this message. What I don't know, yet, is how this fits in with my hypnosis.

We walk in and Dianne greets us. I am relieved. She has a beautiful vibe and I feel safe with her. The three of us walk into her therapy room. I briefly tell her that I have had life-long communications with ETs and recently had an experience in Roswell which I must understand better. I tell her a few of my memories since childhood. She says I have the clearest recollection of anyone she has met.

I lie on the massage table, Patrick sitting beside me ready to take notes. There is soft music playing. I feel my awareness entering another dimensional realm and the music is distracting. I ask Dianne to turn it off and she does. She begins to lead me into a meditative state, but I get there before she finishes.

She sits right behind my head, taking notes. I give her permission to ask what she wants and to guide our interaction. Her questions are not leading. I like that she allows me to move freely through my experiences. She simply asks questions, like an inquisitive reporter.

The following represents the information divulged during my hypnosis session. I have represented it the best I can, for I go from one memory to another very quickly. The session lasts one hour and fifteen minutes and I talk the entire time. With the use of Dianne's notes, Patrick's notes, and my recall, here is what happened.

Within minutes of falling into the state of hypnosis, I start to cry. Dianne asks me why I am crying. I am so overwhelmed, I cannot answer quickly. The love I feel is making it difficult for me to speak. When our senses are overwhelmed, sometimes we release the excess energy through tears. I explain that I am feeling a tremendous amount of unconditional love and it feels amazing.

I see a group of people looking at me. I am unable to make out how many of them there are. Upon closer inspection, they are not human but resemble humans very much. They have human-like bodies, except their arms are a little longer, with faces like humans. They are wearing blue jumpsuits with a large inverted silver triangle on the front of their suits. There are males and females and I understand that they represent a larger group of themselves. They are similar to a senate.

Through tears, I say, "I miss them." I refer to them as "my group" and "my people." They are standing, looking at me as I look at them.

"I'm a little mad at them," I announce. The group explains to me, telepathically, that there was a vote and three people were chosen. The chosen ones had freedom to say yes or no. I was one of the three voted for the "mission" and I agreed to go. I said yes to coming to Earth for investigative purposes. My purpose in this lifetime is to observe the destruction humans are creating and to maintain hope.

"Something went wrong. It was harder than we all thought," I say. I understand that none of us, meaning me and my people, thought that Earth's reality would be as difficult as it is. None of us knew how easy it is to succumb to the pressures and societal dictates leading humans to grapple with creating a meaningful and prosperous life.

Even though I have been to Earth many times before, this particular mission was to be an easier experience due to the particular time I chose to come. Earth is undergoing a dramatic transition and sits on the edge of two future realities. Earth can move towards a peaceful, loving reality or continue to move towards a combative, deathly reality. Due to the 'New Age' movement, global recognition of UFOs, and the dilution of the stigma associated with meditation and inter-dimensional communication, my trip here was not predicted to be as difficult, frustrating, and confusing as it has been.

"What is the name of their planet or their name?" Dianne inquires.

"Sartori," I reply. They are from a star system called Sartori. It is not one planet, it is a system of stars.

The group apologizes to me and I can feel their sympathy towards my struggles. I wonder who exactly am I? Why was I one of the three chosen? What qualified me to be picked for this mission? These questions are not answered for other information is coming quickly and I want to express all of it to Dianne and Patrick. I am aware of both of them in the room. I am aware I am in the room. Going under hypnosis does not make you lose touch with your reality. You know who you are, you know what you are saying, and afterwards, you remember what you said.

Some are afraid of hypnosis for they feel they will lose control over themselves. It is not like that at all. You feel in control. If Dianne had asked me to take my clothes off and run across the street, I would have said no. It feels like you are watching a TV with your eyes closed, one which not only transmits images but transmits emotion, as well. As the viewer, you are in control of the experience.

My people continue to telepathically tell me there are millions of people on Earth doing the same work I am. There are millions who are representatives of their out-of-this world families and are diligently working to maintain hope within humans and to heal them, animals, and Earth.

As I sense my people leaving, I cry. I don't want them to go. I long for them. I miss them terribly. I feel my mission is a big one and I need their support. It is understood that I always have their support and can call on them telepathically and inter-dimensionally for aid. Knowing this eases my sadness for their departure.

I explain that there are many planets and many entities. We are not the only ones destroying ourselves. The whole galaxy is hurting. As I and millions of others do our work to maintain hope and offer healing, this effects the energy of Earth which, in turn, effects the energy of the entire galaxy. My mission is not just to heal Earth but the entire galaxy. That is why there are millions of us doing this. It takes many to heal Earth and provide hope for its inhabitants.

I feel frustration as I try to explain how many planets there are and how many civilizations there are. There are no

words to explain the complicated interaction between the unlimited amount of ETs and galaxies and dimensions. I say that I am
"fractionalized." Many have parts of me. My whole has been
polyped off and shared with many groups of ETs.

"It got out of hand," I say referring to my fractionalization. I agreed to be fractionalized to meld with many ETs. I say
that I have more control now. I am not as willing to give a fractionalized part of me away anymore. The Greys are part of my
fractionalization. I say they want a part me of me; they want my
DNA. I agreed to give them a part of me and this was not part of
my mission.

Dianne asks me to call upon the Greys. They enter. I am
staring face to face with a large head which resembles an insect
and I am very upset. I start kicking, trying to kick it away. It
scares me. It makes me feel like I have no control over myself.
Dianne asks me why they want a part of me.

"For three reasons. First, because I have the DNA of Sartori. Second, I can easily express emotion. Third, I am nice. I let
them do it to me," I respond.

Dianne asks if I can talk with a leader or the head of this
particular group of Greys. When I ask, the same bug-like Grey
remains. Dianne asks me if I can make an agreement that they
leave me alone. I tell the leader that I don't like them and I ask
them to leave me alone. It says it will abide by my request. I

don't feel like it is telling the truth. I feel as if it is talking to me as you would a child, telling me only what I need to hear to calm me down, whether it is the truth or not.

Dianne inquires about the baby in the test tube. "The baby is one of millions, billions. There are millions of humans creating billions of these hybrids." I answer. These babies are super-human. They are engineered to possess the best qualities of humans. These babies are presenting a huge problem within the galaxies.

"There is a huge issue about whether these babies should be killed or not," I report. There is a fear within the galaxies that these billions of super-human babies may be used for hate," I say.

I telepathically understand that these billions of babies, most of whom are kept in a state of "sleep," will be activated for later use. Some are living on Earth now but most are not. If this planet destroys its inhabitants, these babies will be supplied to repopulate this planet. Whether we destroy ourselves remains to be seen. The effects of our destruction will resonate throughout the galaxies, through the dimensions. We are being watched and aided as much as possible without interrupting our free will so that we do not destroy ourselves or the planet. However, the ultimate course Earthlings take is completely a function of their desire.

Dianne asks about our Roswell incident. At Roswell, I saw images, in my mind's eye, of myself talking with Greys. What were we talking about? The meeting in Roswell was to urge me not to write the book I was writing. The book was about self-love and how it holds the power to create one's life. They wanted to make a deal with me. They told me if I don't write the book, they could promise me notoriety. I am not propelled by celebrity, so I was not interested in such a deal.

After my session, I find in Patrick's notes the following entry: "Book: Identity of true essence." It is underlined. I don't remember what it refers to. Is it a book I am going to write?

My people are back. They are apologizing. This time, there are other ETs with them. They are blue, tall, skinny, scary-looking, but they are nice. The Blues are just watching and they are benevolent. Once again, I try to explain, with frustration, the variety of ETs and the unlimited amounts of them. There are many different Federations and "It all goes into infinity," I say.

I explain that there are hybrids amongst the children, politicians, and entertainers on Earth. Some are drug addicts, some are bad. I understand that the addictions and "badness" comes from not understanding their true identity. I say that I am going to meet these people. They will find me and it will happen soon.

"I just entered a time warp," I continue, "I am traveling and I hear Mozart. I am in a huge room and Mozart, himself, is playing. I am mad. I don't want to be there." I explain that the people in the room are fake and stupid.

"Why am I so fucking rich?" I ask with disdain. I am married to a rich man who got his money from his father. I was told to marry him. I want to leave these people. I run away at the age of 23 and don't go back. I laugh as I say I ran away, proud of what I did. I died at 43.

At this time we are forty-five minutes into my session. I then say, "I was the most happy when I could heal. That was my purpose. It is nothing special. It is just normal."

I begin to get upset and frustrated and do not know why. All of a sudden, I feel suspended in water and am washed with peace and joy.

"I am in the ocean," I say smiling. "I am so happy. I am an energy in the ocean. I love it."

Quickly I switch to another reality. "I am in a room," I announce. "I'm in jail. God damn it. I just keep doing it to myself because I speak my mind. I'm a man. I have been in prison seventeen times." I say this with a smirk on my face for I find it amusing.

"The government is all assholes," I continue. "It is 1532. It's okay. They feed me." I am an aristocrat in a territory of England. I say that the government is corrupt and that the common people are completely ignored. The irony is that my relatives are wealthy and work in the government. Because of my family ties, I cannot be harmed so to try to keep me quiet, they keep putting me in jail but only for a few days. I feel that I am free to speak knowing that my imprisonment is a joke and I will not be hurt or held for a long time. I see myself as a man wearing expensive clothing and sitting on a small wooden stool in the center of a small stone room. The government cannot jail me for long due to my connections.

"I am seeing a light," I say. "It feels good." I continue to explain that I have had many lives and that I mentally tortured myself.

"Humans are so disconnected," I continue, "Humans are so lost. I did not realize this when I agreed to be a human."

Then my attention turns to Patrick. "Patrick is my guardian. He was sent to me because I needed him so much. He doesn't know it, but he was guided to me." Then I give Patrick a personal message.

It is now one hour into my session and Dianne asks who visited me when I was a little girl. He was an ET who visited my mother, my sister, and my father. My mother and sister were scared, but my father talked to him. The ET is part of a Galactic Federation and there are many multi-stellar and multi-dimensional Councils. The ET, who visited me when I was a little girl, was head of a Council and he never was a human. The Councils are learning that the mission has been hard for all of us.

I say the final words, "We are retreating so we can be ourselves. Patrick needs a break." And I know that the session has ended.

Upon opening my eyes, I remember everything. I am very pleased with the information that came forth. Dianne and I talk a few minutes about my past lives and about the Greys. I really cannot converse too much. I am overloaded mentally, physically, and spiritually. I feel dizzy as if I am buzzing. We exchange good byes and thank yous.

Patrick and I walk to the car and sit quietly. I don't feel I am completely back to being myself. Patrick asks if I want to go to Luray Caverns. I want to go. While we tour the beautiful Caverns I take the little, green Grey toy we bought at the Roswell gift shop out of my purse. I situate him so that he appears in the corners of some of the photos we take, as if it lives in the Caverns peeking into our photos. This amuses us for a while. During the long drive home from Luray Caverns, we are both quiet. Patrick is processing what he witnessed and I am processing what I know.

When we get back to Capitol Hill, we don't talk about what happened for several days. I wait until I feel like talking and I provide the same freedom for Patrick. Our realities have shifted. We need time to integrate the experience to figure out how this will shape our lives individually and as a couple.

HEART LOGIC

About a week after my session with Dianne, Patrick walks into my office and sits down. He is ready to talk about my hypnosis. I listen as he provides details and expresses his views in a very open manner. Logical Patrick knows I was not faking it. He says my speech patterns and voice changed several times and I used words I have not used before. He knows the emotions I expressed were real to me. Even though he can not logically explain how hypnosis works, he knows something rare and real happened.

His feedback is very valuable to me. I am not aware of my speech and voice changing. I remember using the word "fractionalized" which is a new word for my vocabulary. However, when I used the word during the hypnosis, it did not feel like a foreign word. It felt like a word I knew well. We both agree that it was an extraordinary event, answering some of my life-long questions while creating many others. My biggest question now is *What am I supposed to do with all this information?*

I decide I don't want anything to do with the Greys. I throw away all the alien toys we bought at the International UFO Museum's gift shop. Even the Grey sticker I put on my iPad beside my NASA sticker, I cover over with another sticker. I want nothing around to remind me of the Greys. I do not want to think of them at all. I hope that if I put them out of my mind, they will be out of my life.

As far as coming to terms with the information from my hypnosis, it is all still settling in. What is most important right now is packing up our house and driving to the Inner Banks of North Carolina. We decide to move a few minutes outside of Oriental, the sailing capital of North Carolina. Patrick has started his early retirement and we are ready to leave D.C., to live along the water, and sail.

He is retired, but I am not. I will continue my practice doing Soul Purpose Readings, writing, and speaking about conscious manifestation. Since I conduct the sessions via FaceTime, Skype, or telephone, I can work from anywhere in the world. I intentionally create a business for myself with a lot of freedom. When I ended my second marriage, I was on a quest for freedom: freedom of thought, freedom to speak, freedom to be as I choose to be. My entire life I squelched all of those freedoms in order to appease others.

This move is heart-wrenching for me, as much I want to move. I have to leave my best friends, my mother, and my sister and her family. I am leaving the Mid-Atlantic region of the U.S. which has been the backdrop for the most important events in my life. I have adopted Mid-Atlantic attitudes and belief systems. I am moving to the Bible Belt and that is a very different place with very different attitudes than mine.

Regardless of the emotional difficulty, I am ready and excited for it. One of my very best girlfriends hosts a going away party for us. She took me under her wing after I left my second husband. She listened to my dating stories, took care of me when I was sick, invited me to parties, had me over for dinner, gave me gifts, helped me move, and loved me like a cherished family member. I cannot thank her enough.

My mother cooks a lot of Turkish food for the party, and my best friends come. I cry during most of it. My tears are not enough to keep me from adventure. As an infant I went on an adventure across continents. Adventure is in my blood. I am making the move because my heart tells me it is the right thing to do. I have no idea what is in store for us in North Carolina, but I have strong faith. I can hear my heart and I have learned to listen to it and follow its guidance. I have no worries that I am doing the wrong thing. The heart always tells the truth.

I know we are moving towards something good, but we have no idea how much our lives will change once we get to the small town of Arapahoe, North Carolina.

YOU HAVE THE RIGHT TO TALK TO ALIENS

MARKED WITH AN X

September 16, 2017, Arapahoe, North Carolina

"Patrick! I think something just bit my butt! Will you look at it?" I yell over my shoulder from the kitchen sink, washing newspaper-packed dishes. Only two days ago, we moved from Capitol Hill to the Inner Banks of North Carolina. We went from a city townhouse minutes from the U.S. Capitol Building to a country house at the end of a dirt road. We exchanged dirty air, concrete vistas, and over-populated living conditions for fresh air, water-side vistas, and a population of 535.

"Sure," Patrick replies. After living with me for two years, my odd requests are now ordinary for him.

I dry my hands and walk to the living room couch. As I look at the beauty of Beard's Creek through the long row of windows lining the living room, I am filled with peace. Historians and folklore believe the creek is named after the pirate Blackbeard, whose family lived here and who was beheaded on the nearby island of Ocracoke. Despite the violence Blackbeard symbolizes, his namesake creek is the epitome of tranquility. I am unaware that the calm will give way to alarmed confusion in the next thirty seconds.

I giggle to myself as I arrive at the couch, finding it funny that I am requesting an ass inspection. I bend over and allow Patrick's examination. I wait for a response, but there is silence. I wait. More silence.

"Well? Did something bite me?" I finally pierce the dead air, anxious for what he is to say next.

"There is a bug bite," he says and pauses. His voices softens, "And there is an X mark." My heartbeat accelerates. Fear enters my body and slithers through me.

"What?! An X?! Take a picture," I demand. I pull up my pants and stare at the digital photo. There is an X over an inch wide comprised of small, red dots. The dots look as if they are burned into my skin forming a very precise pattern. The red dots form scabs, flush against my flesh. Staring at the photo, I am frozen. My reality, as I know it, is wiped away. I have a new bizarre reality, one where mysterious markings show up on my body. Being in a state of confusion is hard to explain. It is as if no one else exists, there is no time, and nothing is as it seems. I am disoriented. I can't talk.

As the tears well up in my eyes, Patrick feels useless in his ability to protect me and soothe me. He gently asks, "What can I do for you?" I have no answer.

For the next two days, I search the house, the yard, the cars looking for the chair or the pants or the fabric or the something capable of burning nine perfect little red circles into my body without me feeling it. I come up empty handed. My mind, insisting on finding an answer, goes somewhere I don't want it to go. I can't go there. I can't open that door. It is too scary.

I try to forget about it, but I can't. First the rectangle and now this X. Dreams since childhood begin to play like video snippets in my mind's eye. Could it be that my weird, intense dreams are not dreams but real experiences? Are my dreams actual memories? Who marked me with an X? And why?

YOU HAVE THE RIGHT TO TALK TO ALIENS

FIRST X ON LEFT CHEEK

MARKED TWICE

September 25, 2017, Arapahoe, North Carolina

My eyes pop open and I am wide awake. I am thrust into 3D reality. I do not awaken slowly, as I often do. Instead, I go from sleep to awake in a split second. As I lie there, the memory of what happened seeps into my awareness. I get out of bed, fearing what I will find on my body.

I go downstairs to make coffee as my memory of last night gains clarity. It has been nine days since the first X. I patiently wait for Patrick to come downstairs. Almost always Patrick gets up first but not this morning.

I hear him walk to the bathroom. I want to run up there and demand another inspection. I tell myself to be patient because I dread what I might discover within the next few minutes. Finally, Patrick comes downstairs, says his good morning, gets his cup of coffee, and sits on the couch with me. I barely give him time to take his first sip before I ask, "Patrick, did you notice me missing from bed last night?"

"No."

"Did you have any strange dreams or see anything weird in the room last night?" I try to ask calmly, but my pulse is racing.

"No." His face shows increasing concern. He knows something happened.

As I describe to him where I was and what happened to me, it feels unreal and very real at the same time. This time, I am not worried about my sanity, as I have my entire life. This time, I am worried about how our lives will change. Will Patrick still want to be with me? Is this too much for him? Does this scare him? These thoughts are forefront in my mind, not whether last night's travel was real or not. *I know it was real.*

I begin to tell him where I was last night. I was in a bed, similar to a hospital bed. I was lying on my right side. My arms tight beside my body, my legs stretched out. I couldn't move my arms and legs. I was in a sterile-looking room that had no furniture other than the bed. I sensed something behind me. I looked over my left shoulder and there was a Grey standing behind me doing something to my body. I was terrified. We looked into each other's eyes. It was like looking into two pools of black oil. No words were exchanged between us, verbally or telepathically. I sensed a neutral feeling from the Grey, it was not hostile nor sympathetic, but I was still scared.

The Grey had several large wrinkles on its face between its forehead and nose. Its skin color was a mix of gray and tan. It had large, slanted black eyes, a small pug nose, and a very tiny mouth like a short slit. I also knew something I had not known in my other ET trips. I was on the Moon. Then, my eyes popped open and I am in our bed.

After quickly describing my event, I utter the words I have been dreading all morning, "Patrick, check my butt."

Once again the inspection begins, and once again there is silence. My heart is going to explode out of my chest and my stomach is flipping.

"Is there an X?" I ask, hoping the answer is no.

"Yes."

"Another one? A second one?" I begin to panic.

"Yes. On the right side. Directly across the other X." His voice dripping with incredulity. I sit on the couch looking at the digital photo unable to speak. I search Patrick's face for a clue as to whether he is going to leave me. He says nothing.

In his eyes, I see him hunt for a logical explanation. Patrick has been searching for logical explanations since meeting me. Because of what I do for a living, what happened to us in Roswell, what he witnessed in my hypnosis session, and the two X's, he cannot come up with any logical theories. So, he likes to say, "That is strong circumstantial evidence, Sev." That is my logical boyfriend. He is a good counter-balance for me.

I stare at another X. It looks just like the last one. It is a red X made up of small red dots and is directly across from the other X. Both X's are low on my butt, close to where my legs start. I cry. After the fear settles, I bounce off the couch and pace the living room.

"I need help," I declare to Patrick with tears in my eyes. "I need someone to help me process this. I cannot do this alone." I must get help or else I am going to lose my mind.

Who do I always go to when I need help? My best girl-friends. I choose five of them who are also in the field of spiritu-al and energetic work. One by one, I send them the pictures of the X and tell them the stories. Telling them makes me feel a lit-tle better. I decide to file it all away in the back of mind and go about my day to day life. I have faith that, with time, my answers and explanations will come. I need to be patient.

I go to sleep wondering what will happen to me during the night. I feel like something else has control over me and is using me for its advantage. I feel abused. I know this feeling well.

For three months, I try my best to act like nothing hap-pened. Then one day, in the beginning of January 2018, I decide to start the new year by divulging my secret. I compose a letter, include a picture of an X, and send it to three internationally-known UFO experts, two women and a gentleman. I get no re-sponse from two of them. One responds a week later letting me know she received my letter and will get back to me, but she does not.

The act of writing the letter is cathartic and very important to my growth and processing of my experiences. Every little step is a big step for me when it comes to healing myself, so the lack of response does not upset me.

One month later, I get a text message from my friend, Elizabeth, suggesting I watch the movie *Unacknowledged* by Dr. Steven Greer. While Patrick is not home, working on his newly-purchased catamaran, I watch the movie. It lights a fire within me. Something washes over me and I am driven to take action.

When the movie ends, I get up from the couch and walk to my desk. At my computer I think to myself, "I have to email my letter to someone, but to whom?" I hear "MUFON" in my head. I go to its website and learn the Mutual UFO Network is internationally recognized and one of the oldest UFO research organizations in the world.

I send my letter to two MUFON field researchers in North Carolina and to Kathleen Marden, the Director of Experiencer Research at MUFON. Kathleen is also on the Board of Directors of the Edgar Mitchell Foundation for Research into Extraterrestrial and Extraordinary Encounters (FREE). She has written many books on the topic of UFOs and has a chapter in FREE's newest book, *Beyond UFOs: The Science of Consciousness and Contact with Non-Human Intelligence.*

Within three days, I hear back from all of them. Kathleen has never seen markings like this and wants to talk with me. Validation! I am going to get help and answers. I pray their attention brings me relief.

Due to Kathleen's busy schedule with writing books, conducting research, and lecturing, her team of investigators provide one-on-one support. If you would like to speak with someone at MUFON regarding your ET contact experience, please visit www.mufon.com. Scroll down to Experiencer Research Team. Follow the links and complete the online questionnaire. A member of the team will contact you.

Kismet brought me to Kathleen's attention. I ask Kathleen if we can talk via FaceTime or Skype. I feel safer seeing her face since I am divulging such personal information. She agrees and we Skype for an hour and a half. This meeting is the most important discussion for me in coming to terms with my lifelong ET contact. I cannot fully express how grateful I am for Kathleen's attention and support.

She believes my ET contacts are legitimate. She shares my interest in the multi-dimensional aspects of abductions. We agree some ET contacts do not happen in linear Earth time. Many abductions happen in a time warp or portal.

I ask her what I should do with this information. I tell her I see myself, in my mind's eye, talking on a stage or to groups of people about ET contact. I tell her I ponder the idea of writing a book. We talk about this at length. Our conversation ends with me leaning towards not writing a book. She never tells me not to write one though. I remain uncertain as to my role in all this. Am I supposed to come out? Am I to help other experiencers?

I have heard stories of the U.S. government bothering people who are verbal about their ET contact by tapping their phones, following them, or the Men in Black knocking on their door. This is all very scary to me. The last thing I want to do is fight with the U.S. government concerning ET disclosure.

A few days before my meeting with Kathleen, I call my mother. "I have something important to tell you," I begin. My heart is beating quickly. I am nervous to spill the beans to my mother. I am unsure of her reaction.

I slowly begin to tell her all of it. I tell her the whole story since my childhood. She listens. She believes me. She is worried for me. The relief I feel is enormous. I tell her I have a Skype call with the Director in a few days and will call her afterwards.

As promised, I call my mother right after my conversation with Kathleen. I cannot share most of what was said, but I do tell her that I don't think I am going to write a book. I am not sure what I am going to do with the information I have and all my stories, but I am in no hurry to figure it out right now. I have been in North Carolina for a little over four months, and I want to explore the beautiful state, relax, do my Soul Purpose Readings, and begin my new life with Patrick.

A few minutes into the phone call with my mother, the phone line goes dead. I am using a land-line, for our cell reception isn't very good out here in the "boonies." I find this super odd. I text Patrick and ask him if we paid the phone bill. It is paid, he tells me, and has no idea why it would die. The phone-line is dead for about fifteen minutes. This freaks me out. I cannot say it is the government listening in on my phone call, but the timing is so interesting that my fear is intensified. So far, the line has not gone silent again.

Fear. This has been the reoccurring theme in my life. Fear of not being a good daughter, wife, sister, employee, business owner, friend, boss, etc. Through years of deep exploration into my heart and mind, I have released the need to appease others, but now this comes up. Now I have fear regarding the Greys and the U.S. government.

This must be my last hurdle. The last giant leap I need to make in order to release fear from my life and to be my authentic self. I know I must heal the fear and abuse still lingering in my body. If I don't, I will hold onto these debilitating energies and my life will reflect it. If I don't face these feelings head on I will not have peace. I never thought my last push would be to release my fear of aliens and the U.S. government, the latter which fiercely protects the truth of our inter-galactic reality.

YOU HAVE THE RIGHT TO TALK TO ALIENS

Grey behind me
folds of skin on his
forehead

DRAWING OF GREY
STANDING BEHIND ME

95

YOU HAVE THE RIGHT TO TALK TO ALIENS

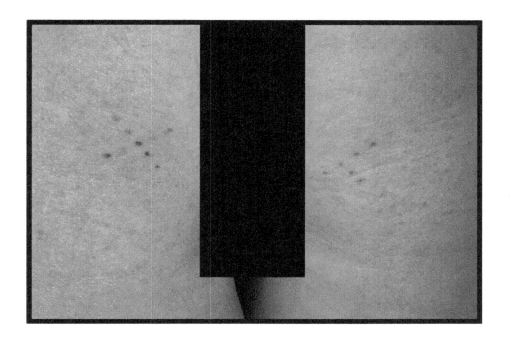

SECOND X ON RIGHT CHEEK

FIRST X STILL VISIBLE

TIME WARP

Alien life is not bound to our 3D reality. ETs can travel without the constraints of time, as we know it. This means contact with ETs often happens outside the limitations of Earth time. There are vortexes of energy which do not adhere to our laws of time and gravity. These vortexes are known as time warps, portals, or wormholes. These are doors between the multi-dimensions. ETs enter and exit through these doors, sometimes taking you with them.

Some of my ET contacts are through these portals. My body is taken through a time warp and replaced back into Earth time. To someone watching me, it would not appear as if I left at all. I can enter a time warp and be back so quickly, it doesn't look like I left. This is mind-blowing stuff.

How do I know I enter time warps or portals? I knew I was on the Moon when I received the second X. It took the Apollo 11 mission three days to get to the Moon. I never disappeared for three days. Maybe you can't believe I was on the Moon. Okay, but I was in a sterile room on a bed resembling a hospital bed. My bedroom does not look like that. I was transported somewhere, came face-to-face with an alien, marked with an X, and came right back, defying the physical rules of Earth.

How does my physical body enter a time warp or portal? My vibration is altered. You are energy vibrating at a certain frequency. ETs have the ability to change your vibration, so you can move through solid objects as is often described in alien abductions. Experiencers have reported moving through a wall or the roof. ETs change your vibration so you can enter another dimension. Think of how Spock's body seems to disintegrate and appear somewhere else when he declares, "Beam me up, Scotty."

In explaining this to you, I know I raise a lot of questions. I do not have answers to all the questions. All I know is what my personal experience is and I don't need to be able to explain it to know that it is real. I can't explain how my cat, Zulu, popped into my dream to tell me she was stuck in the closet, but it happened for real. I ask you to suspend your logical belief system. In doing to, you may be surprised at how much more you discover about yourself and the world.

The mental struggles I go through in accepting my ET contact is directly related to my need to provide proof. I have been brainwashed into thinking without proof, something does not exist. Considering all the supernatural events in my life, you would think I was beyond needing logical proof, but I wasn't. I thought the only way I can have people believe me is to give them hard, irrefutable proof. I was stuck on people believing me. It no longer matters to me if you believe me. I know what happened and your belief in my experience is not necessary for me to know the truth.

Does time warp travel happen only when you are asleep? No. However, when you are in slumber, your energy is different. Your mind is at rest. You are better suited for frequency alteration which makes it possible for you to be transported through inter-dimensional portals.

The Greys told me there are millions of people involved in the hybridization efforts. This means millions of people are traveling through time warps or portals and most don't even know it.

There is a way to alter our physical makeup so we can transcend the laws of Earth to enter another reality. When scientists claim that time travel is not possible because our bodies cannot handle it, that is not correct. Millions of us are already time traveling through time warps and surviving.

YOU HAVE THE RIGHT TO TALK TO ALIENS

SERENDIPITY

In only a few months' time, I have gone from fearing the government to defiantly insisting I have the right to write about my life. I have gone from worrying what others think, to looking people in the eye and telling them I have had ET contact. All along the way, there have been people helping me tell my truth.

My messages of support have come through a variety of people and various circumstances. We have angels all around us. They appear in the most unexpected ways providing guidance and direction. They speak through strangers, clients, family, co-workers, and friends.

I share with you a few of my magical meetings which have caught my attention. As I reflect on my life to write this book, I recognize the Earthly angels who have come to me, offering me support and validation. There are many more than the ones I write about.

Your life is shaped by synchronistic events, providing support and validation that you are moving in the direction of your personal fulfillment. These are not accidental meetings. These are intentional connections through the multi-dimensions.

An angelic message from beyond takes shape while I am in college. My family and I are invited to a party in a mansion near the Loyola University campus. The area surrounding Loyola is a beautiful and affluent area of Baltimore City. We do not know the host, for a mutual friend invites us. I have no idea, and neither does my family, who the host's father is. Decades later, the father delivers a message to me from beyond the grave.

Fast forward thirty-five years. While Patrick and I are in Hawaii, the mutual friend visits us on Kauai. One morning, she tells me she dreamed of General Twining, who is the father of the host of the party she invited us to. She has never dreamed of him before. When she tells me this, I hear a voice in my head say he has died.

"Did he die?" I ask her.

"I don't know," she replies.

"Let's google," I say. We learn that he left Earth thirty-four years prior. I then read something which stops me in my tracks.

"He was at Roswell?" I ask surprised.

"Yes. He knows what happened at Roswell." I knew this was no coincidence. The only time the General visits my friend, in her dream, is in my home. My friend is the messenger of an all important communiqué for me. I learn that General Twining was a four-star General in the Air Force. He was also the Chief of Staff of the Air Force (1953-1957) and President Eisenhower appointed him Chairman of the Joint Chiefs of Staff (1957-1960).

As I keep googling, I discover that General Twining was part of the Majestic 12, which was a secret group comprised of government and military personnel together with scientists. It was formed in 1947 by President Truman. This is the same year as the UFO crash in Roswell. The aim of the secret group was to recover and investigate alien spacecraft.

The more I google, the more I learn about General Twining. His memo, dated 1947, is one of the most famous government memos about Roswell there is. General Twining wrote a memo to Air Force General George Schulgen about the crash site at Roswell. There is lots of information in the memo. Basically, General Twining claims flying discs were recovered.

There are questions about the credibility of General Twining's memo. There is also disbelief that the Majestic 12 even existed. There is so much evidence proving and disproving ET-related incidents that it is hard to discern what the truth is.

Another angelic message comes through a client. One week before we are to move to North Carolina, a new client comes to my home for a Soul Purpose Reading. She lives in Baltimore and insists on having her reading in person. I tell her I am in D.C., so we can do FaceTime or Skype. She wants it in person and is willing to drive. It can be a long drive battling D.C. traffic, but if she wants to do that, I welcome her.

About fifteen minutes before she arrives, I sit in the living room with my iPad and start googling around. I come across a video, on youtube, of a woman talking about hybrids. Her name is Delores Cannon and I do not know of her. I listen and she blows me away. She is validating everything I have been experiencing. She talks about the hybridization efforts of ETs and humans. She says people around the world are telling their personal stories about it. Before I can listen to the entire program, my client arrives.

She sits on the couch and, without any word from me, tells me she thinks she is a hybrid and I am one too. I smile and try to talk, but there are too many words flooding from my brain to my mouth. It takes several seconds to compose myself.

"This is unbelievable," I tell her. "Do you know where I am going tomorrow? I am going to an alien abduction hypnotist to get some answers as to what happened to us in Roswell. And right until you arrived, I was listening to Delores Cannon talk about hybrids."

We keep in touch since her reading, just so we can connect energetically and share what is happening in our lives. Talking to her is like talking to a sister who extends a lifeline of nurture and validation.

A stranger at a party delivers angelic support, as well. In D.C. I attend a crowded party. As I stand by the food table, a young man stands beside me. He says his name is Steven and we strike up a conversation. I don't know how this happens, but we start talking about aliens and hybrids and UFOs. I do not easily talk about these topics with people I know, let alone strangers.

We are so engrossed, we sit down and talk for a long time. He has seen many UFOs and, since our meeting, sends me pictures and videos of them that he has personally taken. I marvel at how often he sees them. He sends me links to radio shows and other information that he thinks I will find interesting. His help and support are valuable to me and keep me focused on my truth.

Angelic guidance appears through my new neighbors, here in Arapahoe, N.C. Of all the places to move to, we move onto a street where two neighbors have UFO knowledge. One neighbor does not like to talk about what happened to her. Another neighbor, Gary, has a passionate interest in it and, as I have been told, "...has read every book there is about it." There is also a gentleman living nearby who has had personal experience with a spaceship. He sent a written brief to the U.S. Congress about what he saw while working on a military vessel. He visits me in my home for three hours and believes my ET contacts are real.

Making the decision to move here more validating, I have been asked to consult on a TV series about the mystical qualities of this area. The first second I laid eyes on the lovely lady writing the script, I heard in my head "family." When she laid eyes on me, she was surprised at how much I look like her mother. We have been here less than one year and the doors are flying open with opportunities regarding my ET experiences and knowledge.

It feels like we were guided to this house, to this street, to this neighborhood, to this state. I recently discovered North Carolina is in the top ten list of states with the most UFO sightings.

Often the hardships of life take the focus away from the all-important synchronicities of life. I pay close attention to these very special events. They are loud messages signaling that you are headed in the right direction with your life. When you are out of synch with the true purpose of your life, your reality reflects it. Life seems like a drudgery, a mechanical construct of going to work and going to sleep and not much in between.

When you are achieving your purpose for this lifetime, the entire universe aligns with you and provides a beautiful support system. Life becomes fulfilling and dynamic. You feel creative and stimulated You are healthy and energetic. You are in love with your life.

You are not alone. Ever. There are people out there you don't even know who, one day, will be your angelic messengers of love and guidance. All you have to do is listen to your heart and follow its desires. Then, the brightest beacon of light emerges from your heart illuminating the path for your angelic messengers to find you. You, too, may be an angel for someone.

Sometimes, we don't even realize the impact we have on another person. Our brain doesn't have to know it. The heart knows it. The more you allow human angels to help you, the more helpful you become, in return. Earth feels this energetic transaction and uses this highest frequency of energy, love, to heal itself and all that is on it.

YOU HAVE THE RIGHT TO TALK TO ALIENS

MOZART

It has been eight months since my hypnosis session with Dianne. The session is a pivotal point in my personal growth, for it paves the way to reveal my secrets since childhood. In my personal quest to be the most authentic version of myself, my secrets need to see the light of day. A personal secret does not need to be divulged to others, but it does require you meet it face to face if you want to be your true self. Living in an inauthentic way by hiding secrets, brings frustration, sickness, and dissatisfaction into your life.

I have been processing my session and, as the days pass, my translation of the messages and memories become clearer to me. Since I share my session with you, I will now share my interpretation of it.

My session begins with "my people" appearing. I am overwhelmed with feelings of intense love. I feel love towards them and I feel their love towards me. It is a love which holds no judgement. It feels so pure and so real, that my physical body has a hard time accepting it. It is a love which feels more powerful than any love I have felt on Earth. It is a love which is unconditional. As humans, we thrive for this love, and, unfortunately, it does not exist in abundance on our planet.

I now understand why the Galactic Visitor checked up on me during my childhood. He was making sure I was well enough to complete my mission. I do not think the Galactic Visitor is actually one of my people. I believe he is an overseer for many ET groups who send missionaries to Earth.

On the Galactic Visitor's final visit, I am surrounded by many children. Now, I know the children were also missionaries from various planets and galaxies. I wonder if I will meet the other kids. I have hunch I have met a couple, but this is an area of my reality which needs more clarity and exploration.

There are hybrid missionaries amongst the children, politicians, and entertainers on Earth. Some of them have addictions or exhibit "bad" behavior. Their addictions and bad behavior may stem from not recognizing or understanding their true identity. Ignoring you heart's messages and intuitive knowledge often leads to depression, alcohol and drug abuse, and cruel behavior towards others.

I know that I am going to meet these hybrids. We will find each other. When you live in a way which honors your true identity, you align with others who are doing the same. This is how hybrids find one another, through the path of authenticity.

I believe every human has an ET link. All of us have galactic DNA. The different races of humans represent the variety of races on other planets. The diversity found in our genetic matrix is a replication of the genetic diversity found throughout the cosmos.

Could it be that an Earthling is not originally of Earth? Maybe an Earthling is a mixed bag of life forms from all over the galaxies, living on Earth but not really of Earth.

Scientists have been searching for the "missing link" and cannot find it. Our missing link will not be found in bones buried in the Earth. Our missing link will be found by searching off the planet.

"Sartori," I reply to Dianne's question about where my people are from. My googling attempts to find such a star system have not yielded confirmation that Sartori exists. Then again, we have not discovered most of the stars and planets in our dimension, let alone the other dimensions. Our knowledge of what exists in the cosmos is quite restricted.

I am not sure how I am from Sartori and how I am Sev, at the same time. I don't identify as an ET visiting Earth. I feel very human. However, I do feel a strong connection with other life forms in the universe. I am not clear on how my Sartori self becomes my Sev self. It is not that I don't believe it, I just don't understand it and don't base my self-identity on it.

Since childhood, I have had a fascination with the constellation Orion. It is the first constellation I look for in the night sky. Seeing it makes me feel good, that is the best way to put it. To me, this signals a primal knowing of my connection to interstellar life.

Earth's energy affects other galaxies. Just like a human has an aura, so does a planet. Earth's aura reflects the pain, killing, and fear prevalent on our planet. ETs have a stake in whether Earth heals or not. The missions millions of us have to provide healing and hope to the people of Earth is vast in its scope. The work is done through a variety of venues. Some of us are energy healers, therapists, entertainers, writers, artists, politicians, doctors and nurses, innovators, and scientists. All of us share the common goal of moving Earth into a more advanced and kinder reality.

Some of us are here to help with spiritual awakening while others are here to help with scientific breakthroughs. Some of us are here to present alternative ways of thinking through music, art, and literature. There are also some of us working in governments around the world, trying to break barriers between people, so we can unite as a civilization instead of war with one another.

When I try to explain the enormity of how many planets, life forms, galaxies, and dimensions there are, I get frustrated. It feels like I don't have the words or the capability to express the vastness and unlimitedness of it all.

Right before walking into Dianne's office, I meditate and see a star in my mind's eye. I hear the words, "Eternal star. Multi-dimensional fractal star. Star goes into infinity." I now see how that fits in with my session.

A fractal is a geometric shape where each portion of the whole has the whole within it. For example, the fractal star I saw in my meditation is a star which has an infinite number of smaller stars in it. In other words, no matter how small a piece you cut out of the star, the whole star is reflected in the smallest portion. Fractals continue into infinity.

When I say that I am "fractionalized," I refer to it in terms of giving away a part of me to other life forms. In the hybridization efforts, my DNA is given away to create other living entities. My DNA is a fractal. It is a geometric form which is multi-dimensional. There is no junk DNA. That is science showing its arrogance. Just because we do not understand how the human body works, does not mean the parts we can't understand are useless.

"It got out of hand," I say in the session, referring to my fractionalization. I agreed with many ETs to share my DNA. I say the Greys want a part of me and I agreed to it even though this was not part of my mission. To me, this reflects the same pattern of behavior I have on Earth. I gave parts of myself to my abusers. I gave, they took. I acknowledge I have more control now. That mirrors the control I have on Earth. I don't accept abusive behavior towards me anymore. As I come to terms with this on Earth, I am apparently healing it in my inter-galactic lives too.

When the Greys enter my session, I am filled with fear and feel out of control. I ask the Greys to leave me alone and they agree to, but I don't feel they are telling the truth. After all, they mark me with two X's after my session. A few days after the second X, I enter a meditative state and talk to the Greys from my higher self. I tell them whatever deal I made, I am ending it. It is not about asking but declaring our agreement to be over when the contact stops. Since breaking the agreement through my higher self, the Greys have left me alone

I have not given birth in this lifetime. There was a short period of time in my second marriage when we tried to conceive, but it didn't happen. My entire life, I have been 50/50 with re-spect to having kids. If I have them, great. If I don't, great. I nev-er thought about having non-Earthling kids though.

Knowing that the Greys used my DNA to create hybrid babies does not emotionally affect me. I feel neutral towards my participation in the program. I don't have the need to see the children, hold them, or even know what is going to happen to them. When I looked at the baby in the tube, I felt disconnected from it.

I explain that there are millions of humans who have hybrid babies. They will be used to repopulate Earth if we continue on the current path of self-destruction. Maybe this is why I never had children on Earth. It is very possible that having these hybrid children took away my desire or maybe even my physical ability to have children on Earth. However, I have heard about women who claim to have hybrid, alien babies and human babies at the same time. The reasons I do not have children are many and not solely because I was involved in the hybrid program.

The hybrid babies are super-human. They possess the best qualities of humans. What are the qualities the Greys want? They say they chose me for three reasons. One, because I have the DNA of Sartori. I understand the ETs from Sartori possess the qualities of love, tenderness, and a high level of psychic abilities.

The second reason they chose me is because I easily express emotion, especially love. Patrick tells me he admires my ability to express love for all living things. I have respect for all life. Patrick is skilled at capturing spiders, bees, flies, and wasps from inside the house to free them outside. I do not like to kill. For this reason, I choose not to eat animals. I easily say "I love you." I can say it without the need to hear it back. It is irrelevant to me if someone says it back. I just have the need to express it.

In Roswell, I am told the Grey's have learned about a key ingredient in keeping a race of sentient beings alive: empathy. Without it the race is heartless and uncaring, resulting in a temperament incapable of nurturing a growing population.

The Greys do not want to make robots, they want to make living beings infused with empathy and love. From this perspective, I do not think their hybridization project is created for evil. I do not believe the super-human babies will be used to take over Earth by killing the life on it. If we look at the purpose of the hybrids from the perspective of their ingredients, using them to deliver evil would not result in a successful mission. Robots are the perfect creatures to carry out missions of death and destruction, not beings infused with empathy.

Our militaries try to produce effective death machines from humans. It isn't working well. Look at what these wars do to those who take part in them and to those who are affected by them. Through warring and killing, we have created mental turmoil and produced an imbalance in the natural order of things. Humans are not mass-killing machines. No matter what our government or military want us to believe, the majority of humans can't handle the mental repercussions of killing one another.

The third reason they chose me is because I let them. This gets back to the agreement I made with them and my higher self. Your higher self calls the shots. What makes being a human so difficult is that we have lost the direct communication between the higher self and the heart. There is a pathway between the two and, in Western society, we have been conditioned to cut the pathway or to ignore it.

Your heart is a sensor for your higher self. When your heart feels joy for a person, event, or decision it is because your higher self is in alignment with it. Acting in alignment with your higher self is the easiest way to manifest and create the life you desire.

If I have an agreement between my higher self and the Greys, then why didn't I feel joy and happiness when I made contact with them? My personal filters were in the way, discoloring my reality. Because I looked at everything through the lens of abuse, I allowed that perspective to override any other emotion.

Now, the filter of abuse is removed and I feel very differently about my ET trips. Maybe if I did not react like a stray cat, afraid of the person capturing it to care for it, I may have had very different memories of my ET contacts.

Because no ET race will interfere with our free will, help for our planet comes through the millions of missionaries.

Rather than forcing change from the outside, ETs have decided to help from within the population. This is why there are millions of people, sent from galaxies near and far, to help heal the planet, its people, and its animals.

Some call these people Starseeds or Lightworkers. The most effective Starseeds or Lightworkers are the ones who don't push their ideas on others. For those of us who are here to heal and love, it is paramount to do our work through the construct of acceptance and non-judgment towards others.

I stress that Starseeds, Lightworkers, or humans involved in the hybridization program are not special people. There is no hierarchy when it comes to a person's 'specialness.' Every living being is equally very special.

"I was the most happy when I could heal. That was my purpose. It is nothing special. It is normal," I say. In this lifetime, I am the happiest when I help others heal. I am driven to heal myself too. How can I be an effective healer if I am not healing myself along the way?

I visit two of my lives. In one, I am a woman, married to a wealthy man, and call the other wealthy folk fake and stupid. I see myself at a party where Mozart, himself, is playing. I express my disdain for the people there by asking, "Why am I so fucking rich?"

In this life, I do not hate the rich nor have ill feelings towards them. However, for most of my life I did not care for Mozart's music. I listen to classical music and enjoy going to the symphony. Listening to a live symphony brings tears to my eyes, the music moves me so much. I grew up playing the flute and often played classical music. For some reason, which I never understood, Mozart's music made me uncomfortable. I couldn't logically explain it until now. It is interesting how the likes and dislikes in one life are formed by the experiences of another life. Now, I can listen to Mozart with an open heart and allow his musical creations to heal me.

I am a man in the other life. Once again, wealthy. I am imprisoned seventeen times for speaking my mind, for speaking my truth. Despite the many imprisonments, I do not shut up. The first life with Mozart, I do not speak up, I run away. In the second life, I speak up and face the consequences. There seems to be a thread running through my lives, dealing with speaking up and being authentic. Maybe in this life, I will heal it all by speaking up through this book and not fearing the fallout. I would consider that a successful life for myself.

Patrick is an essential part in my quest for authenticity. In the session, I tell him he was guided to me. He came to help me speak and live my truth. In turn, I help him be the best version of himself too. Patrick has provided me with a beautiful place here by the water and a safe atmosphere to release my mental straight jacket. I spiritually called for him. I was ready for him. If he had appeared in my life earlier than he did, we may not have dated. He came at the exact time I needed him. I am eternally grateful for him.

What happened to Patrick and me in Roswell is what prompted my session with Dianne. I have been thinking about this part of the session the most. It makes more sense to me now than it did at the time of the session. In Roswell, I knew I had a meeting with the Greys. I knew it was about a book I was writing. That was all I could consciously remember. Did they want to help me write it? I was really confused by it. At the time, I was viewing the Greys through my lens of abuse and I wanted nothing to do with them.

I learn that the Greys tried to convince me to write a book other than the one I was writing at the time. I was writing about self-love and how it gives you the power to create your life to your standards. They told me if I write another book, it will be more successful. I felt like they were asking me to make a deal with the devil.

There is a line in Patrick's notes: <u>Book: Identity of true essence</u>. When I saw this in his notes, I did not understand nor remember what it referred to. Now, I know. It refers to *this* book. This is the book about my true essence. I am writing it to help others discover their true essence. In my quest to become my most authentic self, this book must be written. My hope is that it awakens truths within others to practice the alchemy of their personal transformation.

I am writing this book to help me and others become the most authentic versions of ourselves. The expression of our authenticity heals the planet, the people, and the animals. Truth fuels personal, planetary, and inter-planetary transformation from fear to love.

It is through authenticity we show self-love. How could I write the book about self-love when I wasn't being my authentic self? By writing this book, I become the real, genuine me. This book has to come first. When I write from my heart, exposing my secrets, telling my truth, I write a better book, one that people will identify with and one that will reach many more people.

So, I wasn't making a deal with the devil. My lens of abuse distorted things for me. The Greys were not abusing me or trying to mess up my mind. I was the one doing that.

"Humans are so disconnected," I say. "Humans are so lost." I very much believe we are operating on a half empty tank. We don't understand fully how the human body and mind work. This is incredulous to me. We do not know how we work! Despite the lack of this imperative knowledge, we try our best to create happy, fulfilling lives. We don't have all the information we need to find joy easily. That information is kept from us through our own ignorance and through the bully tactics of institutions, businesses, and the government.

We have been in the dark ages regarding who we are and where we come from. Brave people are coming forth to announce the truth in a variety of areas including ETs, our government, Hollywood, pharmaceutical companies, banks, and more.

The more we speak up, the clearer we see who we are and what our purpose is. We are not here to line the pockets of the rich. We are not here to be manipulated by lies, so politicians can create the world *they* want, not what we, the people, want. We are not here to be brainwashed by the medical system so it can push expensive drugs down our throats. We are not here to be myopic, to think humans are the only advanced lifeforms in all the galaxies. We are here to live under the bright light of truth and love. In order to do that, we need all the information not some portion of it.

The big part of our fake story is that ETs aren't real and we don't communicate with them. The truth is we are part of a gigantic inter-galactic system with a variety of life forms and we all interact, visit one another, and aid each other. It is time to wake up. It is time to transform into a physically, mentally, and spiritually advanced society with the knowledge the universe holds.

YOU HAVE THE RIGHT TO TALK TO ALIENS

THE SERPENT

When the X's appear on my back, that changes everything for me. A dream doesn't place strange, inexplicable markings on your body. The proof I was waiting for arrives. It freaks me out, but I am relieved to have evidence that my dreams are not dreams at all but real travels with ETs. The proof doesn't put my mind at rest though. The proof creates many more questions I still cannot answer.

Until the first X, I thought ET abductions happen in a linear fashion, within the parameters of a three dimensional world. I thought I had to see a Grey while awake, in order for the experience to be true. Since I had never seen a Grey with my eyes open, I thought I wasn't having contact with them. I now know my contact is inter-dimensional in nature and time warps or portals are the paths of transportation.

Why two X's on my butt?! I thought it may have to do with my reproductive organs. The Grey's have had access to me since childhood. I don't have conscious memories of them as a child, but I had a very irrational fear regarding them. My feelings bordered on terror. That, to me, is a sign I was having some sort of contact. The baby in the tube was mine, so they have my

DNA and all the reproductive material they need. I do not think the X's are related to my reproductive organs.

Talking about this with MahaDevi, she reminds me that Kundalini energy rests in the first chakra and the Greys could have activated it or deactivated it. To be very brief, because entire books are written about this topic, Kundalini is a Sanskrit word meaning *coiled serpent*. It is the energy of life, the vital force of our existence, the natural source of our power. It sits in the first chakra, in the base of the spine, since birth and leaves the body upon death.

The uncoiling of this energy is potent. Some people never uncoil it in a life time, whereas some partially uncoil it. A human with a completely uncoiled Kundalini is very rare because it creates a disconnect from the physicality of being human. Unfurling it too quickly can be overwhelming to the physical and mental senses. It is like a lightning bolt of energy swiftly moving up all your chakras towards your head. I believe I am in the act of uncoiling it, slowly.

At first, it did not make sense to me that the Greys would activate it because a Kundalini activation is very advantageous. Since I thought the Greys were bad, I leaned more toward the idea that they deactivated it.

Now that I believe the Greys are not evil, I think they activated it. My reality supports this. When Kundalini energy is activated, there is an overwhelming need to know the truth. The desire for inner peace and authenticity is paramount. A dramatic change in outward reality takes place to mirror the changes within. Intuition and other paranormal abilities are heightened. Finding inner truth rules. All of this applies to me now.

Maybe if I didn't experience abuse or powerlessness in my life, I may have had a different attitude about my ET contacts. After all, the Greys were always nice or neutral. They were never hostile or threatening. Now, I see the ETs are not out to hurt me. They are doing a job per our agreement. The job of monitoring me, educating me, and taking the best parts of my DNA to create loving, sentient beings.

Writing this book is a testament to my transmutation, my personal alchemy. I am transforming my victimization, a lower vibratory state of being, into personal power, a higher vibratory state of being.

As far as I know, my Grey travels have stopped. They stopped because I declared it so. I am in control, not they. Every cell in my body wanted it to end and so it did. Why did I stop the abductions? Because I felt I had enough. They got from me what they needed and I got from them what I needed. It was a mutually beneficial relationship and like many relationships, it has ended.

The Greys and I have made an agreement to bust this all out into the open. If I am marked in an inexplicable way, that gets attention. I then share my experiences and help spread the truth. In the process, I conquer my fears of worrying too much what others think. I tap into my personal power to reveal my authentic self. That's my Kundalini rising!

If you are having alien contact and want it to stop, all you have to do is state that you are finished. Don't talk out of both sides of your mouth though. If you want the contact to stop, but you are kinda digging it, it won't stop.

Greys are not evil. There is a type of higher code that exists and life respects it. There is an agreement made between your higher self and with the higher self of every living being. You don't have to understand what the agreement is. In fact, you may not understand it because we are all ignorant as to how the universe works.

When we freely communicate with aliens, there will be no abductions. Maybe the galactic system wants to stop scaring us and unite with us. There are lots of people like me coming out. There is a gigantic momentum swiftly picking up speed regarding the fact that there are intelligent life forms scattered through the galaxies.

The U.S. government cannot brace itself against this giant wave of truth seekers. Our government is cracking under pressure to admit that we have been in contact with ETs for a long time. This is an exciting era in the history of Earth. Our reality is about to shift so severely, that some of us will freak out while others will sigh with relief.

We get knowledge as we are ready for it. We cannot understand more than what we are capable of knowing. ETs will provide us with a lot of answers and truths. Some of it we are not going to like. Some of it will make our lives easier.

If you are reading this book, you know deep inside that there are ETs. You may very well be having contact with them. You may also be part of the reveal. It is getting easier to speak up. There is a lot of support now, the kind that didn't exist a few years ago. Hiding your truth has a negative effect on your life and health. I am not saying you have to write a book or shout it out. I am suggesting you admit your truths to yourself first, and then see what happens. You may be pleasantly surprised because your reality shifts for the better the more authentic you are.

YOU HAVE THE RIGHT TO TALK TO ALIENS

ARE YOU TALKING?

I urge you to investigate your multi-dimensionality. Whether you think you go on ET trips through portals, communicate with ETs inter-dimensionally, or see ETs with your human eyes, please don't think you are crazy. I write this book to save your from that awful mind game.

If you have a "dream" that you can't shake, a nagging feeling that ETs are talking to you, or a deep awareness that you are here to do something big, chances are you are correct. Use your intuition and instincts to help you gain knowledge. You can get answers through meditation, dreams, and hypnosis.

Ask for help. Once you decide that you want to face your ET hunches, you may be surprised at what shows up in your life. I mention the Law of Alignment earlier. This Law provides the way for people, who want to help you, to show up in your life. First, it is necessary that you come out to someone. If you continue to hide, your helpful friends will not show up. Please stop hiding. Don't be afraid. Often we are afraid of things which don't even exist.

If you need clarity, contact the leaders in the field of UFO research. Contact the UFO organizations. If you don't hear back, don't let that discourage you. Keep reaching out. Someone will respond and provide the help you need.

As I begin to tell people I am writing a book about my ET contacts, I am genuinely surprised at how interested people are. I have not been met with any of the reactions I feared. Maybe later, I will be face-to-face with a non-believer who tells me I am crazy, but I think I can handle it.

So far, coming out has been easy and I have met the most interesting people, willing to support me in my quest to be the most authentic version of myself. I was afraid of things which aren't even happening. I was afraid Patrick would leave me. I was afraid some of my friends would turn their backs. All of that was just fake fears in my head.

My coming out was slow. First, I told Patrick, then my girlfriends, then to select clients, and before I knew it, I was writing a book. There are support groups in every state. If there isn't a support group close to you, join an on-line one. It is easy to find support today. The social climate is much more accepting and the internet makes it easy to find information and help.

Maybe you don't think you are in contact with ETs but want to be. I encourage you and caution you. Such interaction needs to come from a place of power. Look at your life. Do you speak up? Do you have healthy relationships? Do you have the career you want? Do you have the lifestyle you want? If you said no to any of these questions, your life is not an expression of your personal power. If you reach out to ETs while expressing fear and powerlessness, you may not be able to handle it.

What do I mean by fear? I mean fear manifested as accepting abusive behavior, keeping yourself small, denying your heart's pleasures, and being afraid to express yourself. I don't mean fear of talking in public, fear of snakes, or fear of needles. I am talking about the kind of fear which prevents you from fulfilling your potential.

When you decide to do the internal work to express your power, there are ETs who can offer you guidance. You can communicate with them in meditations and dreams. Maybe you are ready to channel messages of love and support from spirit guides, angels, and other ETs but not ready to see a Grey. Be careful and ask for only that which you can handle.

I am asked often if there are evil ETs who can destroy someone's life. I say, no. There are no evil ETs, however, there are ETs that feed off of fear. What we call evil, is really a manifestation of fear. The ETs you align with is determined by your energy. If you are a fearful person, not expressing your personal power, you may align with ETs who feed off of your fear; or you may interpret your encounters as negative, like I did. Remember, you are always in charge. "They" are not in control, you are.

If you have started the journey of spiritual awakening and are actively removing fear from your vibratory field, you can align with ETs who want to help you continue with your progress. Interactions with these types of ETs are warm, loving, and transformational.

The kind of friends you attract on Earth is going to be just like the kind of friends you attract in the multi-dimensions. Take a good, hard look at your life. Begin making the necessary changes in your Earth reality before you go looking for new friends in other worlds.

I don't want you to worry about your sanity, as I did. I don't want you to fear being your authentic self, as I have. Don't limit your personal success by adhering to societal rules. Form your own life, in your own way, by listening to your heart. Respect yourself enough to honor your heart. Your heart knows the truth. You heart knows there is life beyond Earth.

We are humans engaged in an inter-galactic reality with ETs. Millions of us are communicating with them and taking trips through time warps or portals with them. I believe it is time to join together and admit the truth to ourselves and to each other. May we understand the highest level of truth we can comprehend. And we can comprehend a lot more than what is being shared with us.

Let's demand the truth. First it must be your truth. Demand to be the most truthful version of yourself you can possibly be. From there, let's collectively demand to know the universal truths kept secret from us. Our new reality is going to have some rough patches. Big institutions are going to crumble. The masses are going to get mad. Devious lies created to keep us down will be illuminated.

You are here to be happy. You came to Earth to spread love to others but most importantly towards yourself. Without loving yourself first, you cannot spread love to others. You cannot give more than what you have. You start loving yourself when you allow yourself to reveal your truths.

I hope, in reading my journey of self-discovery, you feel a spark ignite within you to express your freedom to be. Humans search for freedom because our souls know what it feels like. Our souls are free and we yearn for that feeling. You are a manifestation of the essence of freedom.

If you *think* you are in contact with ETs, do the internal work to reveal the truth. If you *know* you are in contact with ETs, do the internal work to find out why. There is good reason. You have the inter-galactic right to communicate with all life-forms throughout the cosmos. You have the right to experience the truth.

Humans make up a very tiny portion of all the life in the universe. It is natural for you to extend a warm welcome to ETs, for you and they share a basic building block, the "spark of life."

The biggest gift you can give yourself and the universe is the expression of your authentic self. Your genuine self is intergalactic and multi-dimensional with paranormal abilities. And you matter to the universe.

planetsev.com

sev@planetsev.com

Made in the USA
Middletown, DE
20 November 2020